This book is dedicated to 'Charni-bear', Eric and Alison.

And to all those who didn't get to finish their story.

May this book bless you richly.
You are victorious boo!
Love Nicola x

Nicola Morrison

VICTORY IS MY NAME

AUSTIN MACAULEY PUBLISHERS®

LONDON * CAMBRIDGE * NEW YORK * SHARJAH

A CIP catalogue record for this title is available from the British Library.

ISBN 9781035830251 (Paperback)
ISBN 9781035830268 (ePub e-book)

www.austinmacauley.com

First Published 2024
Austin Macauley Publishers Ltd®
1 Canada Square
Canary Wharf
London
E14 5AA

20240724

Acknowledgements

I want to thank all those who made writing this book possible, my amazing and supportive family and friends, but especially my beloved mum and irreplaceable sister. I wouldn't trade you guys for silver or gold! Thank you for your vulnerability, your trust and your selflessness. Thank you for supporting my vision and for allowing me to tell my story without limit or condition, and for loving me unconditionally throughout the process.

I also want to thank the amazing angels without wings that I have encountered on earth along my journey who have made the woman writing this book feel cherished, supported, and capable. The amazing Marky, if I rewrote my life story a thousand times, you would always be in it. Once a formidable trio, now a dynamic pair, I know Charni is still cheering us on, and whenever we are together, I feel her presence most. Thank you for being the true definition of a loyal and trusted friend.

Thank you to Jan, one of the most solid, supportive people I have ever known. You ground me, you motivate me, and you never cease to know just what I need at any given time.

Thank you to Unc and my amazing cousin, two amazing, dependable men in my life who have always stood in the gap for me and held space and made me feel loved, seen and affirmed. I can't begin to count the ways that you and your amazing wives have supported me over the years for which I will be eternally grateful.

A humble thank you to all those who have touched my life that aren't here anymore, who nurtured and shaped the woman that I am today. I'm grateful that our life stories intertwined, albeit too briefly.

Thank you to the many mentors and professional motivators who took a punt and gave me a chance. To David R, Simon, Katie, Judy, Toby and Morwen, thank you for believing in me, for creating opportunities, and for holding the door open for me. You will never know how much it meant to me and continues to mean.

I love you all.

Table of Contents

1. Humble Beginnings   11

2. Forbidden Fruit   20

3 Justice vs Just Is   36

4. Unorthodox   46

5. In the Mirror   51

6. Growing Pains   54

7. Broke   63

8. Re-Invention   79

9. Flatline   94

10. Love Like This Before   107

11. Too Young and Too Dumb   113

12. Adulting   125

13. Evolution   137

14. Room 6045   149

15. Fractures   153

16. When Doves Cry   167

17. Breakthrough   174

18. Adjusting My Crown   179

19. Unprecedented Woman in an Unprecedented Time   183

20. The Ugly Duckling Is Now a Flamingo   190

NICOLA

Latinised version of the Greek name Nikolaos; 'Niko' means victory and 'laos'
means people: 'Victory of the people'.

Attributes of her name:
She is confident and independent.
She has great strength of character,
And is much admired for this.
She is generous to her friends,
And loves her family dearly.
She is patient, considerate and practical.

We delight in the beauty of the butterfly, but rarely admit the changes it has gone through to achieve that beauty.

– Maya Angelou

1

Humble Beginnings

Born on 25 September 1983, in a South London hospital, I'm told I came into the world peacefully and fast. The labour was straightforward, natural, and not too painful (Mum's words not mine). And within 30 minutes of pushing, I was here.

My first official baby photo was taken just hours after I was brought home from the hospital. I'm propped up in a vibrant, burnt orange, knitted sofa in my grandparents' 60s-style living room, looking straight at the camera, holding up my two middle fingers. My mum would later insist that this involuntary pose was a result of me trying to find my mouth with my fingers, which on reflection has some merit, as I would go on to suck said two fingers until the age of nine.

However, I prefer the more humorous narrative that I was displaying to the camera an early indication of the rebellious, non-conformist spirit I possessed within, that was just bursting to come out, that has been ever-present even since the tender age of just one-day-old.

As a baby, I was described as long-limbed and fair. My fair skin would be something that would become a point of conversation for decades to come. Growing up, people would frequently compare my lighter complexion to that of my chocolate-brown siblings, sometimes with a positive inflection, despite the colourist undertones.

Other times, my skin tone yielded more overtly negative comments, masked in jest, which either implied I had been secretly adopted without my knowledge or that my mum had deceptively conceived me with the (assumed White) milkman. Either way, I learnt early on that my skin was different and therefore, that meant I was different.

By all accounts, I was a happy baby. I ate well—fruit, veg, sweet, savoury, you name it, I turned down nothing. I was quick to talk too. At 18 months, I astounded guests at a wedding reception when I announced to the entire room, after my mum had discreetly checked my training pants for any potential leaks, that, "Mummy tickled my bum bum!" causing everyone in the room to fall about in fits of laughter.

I'm told I quite literally slept like a baby, throughout the night and day for hours on end from an early age, which for a mother of two under three, was light relief after two years of virtually no sleep with my older brother. My mum would often retell the story of the time I slept for 14 hours straight and describe how she had been so nervous during my record-breaking 'sleep marathon', that she would intermittently tiptoe over to my crib and peek in, occasionally placing her hand under my nose to make sure that I was still breathing.

As a toddler, I had long, gangly legs, big brown eyes and fine golden-brown curls which lay unceremoniously flat to my head. From a distance, you could be forgiven for thinking my mane was non-existent, but on closer inspection, you would have to appreciate my subtle yet evident blonde fuzz, which lightly adorned my head, for many of my early years.

It took me a little longer than some to grow a full set of teeth too and for a while, my toothy smile consisted of just two baby teeth on the top row of my mouth and two on the bottom. It wasn't long before the nickname Gum-Gum was ascribed to me and thanks to my dad, infamously followed me into my adolescence.

Over the years, I was given many nicknames by family members and friends: Chookie-egg (on account of my thinly covered egg-like crown), Nitala, Atta, Nic-ca-ca, Nic-Nic, Nikki, Nics and Nic Nacs.

It was my dad who gave me my christened name. My mum actually wanted to name me Nicole, although ironically as fate would have it, I probably get called Nicole just about as much as I do Nicola. It's as if the 'la' is just one syllable too much for people to endure, and so they call me Nicole and seemingly assure themselves that it is near enough in the ballpark. I am certain there are millions of Marias being called Marie or Sophias being called Sophie out there, and to them, I truly sympathise with your plight.

Although I was born in South London, I have no recollection of it, as we moved back to Mum and Dad's hometown in North West London by the time I was two years old. Mum felt cut off from everything she knew and desperately wanted to move back to be closer to her family and friends. Dad, less fazed by the prospect of being estranged from loved ones, eventually came around to the idea and agreed to move back to more familiar surroundings.

Mum made her closest brother in age my godfather, on account of his constant protection and adoration for me. With no kids of his own, Unc cherished me as his own. Family members over the years would recite how he used to scoop me up and run out of the room whenever I was in the process of being told off or when anyone would attempt to forcibly remove my fingers from my mouth. Years later, I asked Mum if maybe his devotion to me was because I reminded him so much of her at that age.

Perhaps, my reprimands caused him to reminisce about her defiantly sucking her identical two fingers in the presence of disapproving, tutting elders and witnessing it for a second time had transported him back in time; this time swooping in and coming to my rescue! Whatever the reason, there was an undeniable bond between Unc and I, and it was plain for all to see.

One of my earliest memories as a child was when I was around four years old and we lived in a three-bed, top-floor flat, in a new development in Wembley, called Elliot Close. It was just the three of us, me, Mum and Sean, my older brother. Sean is only two years older than me, although, in the early years, he looked after me as if there were ten years between us. He would often refer to me in social settings as his 'little sister' and took great pride in the duty of looking after me—a self-appointed responsibility he took seriously and assumed virtually as soon as he could walk.

When he was just two and a half years old, to my mum's horror, he carried me out of my crib and into the living room to greet her, announcing as he entered the living room, "The baby woke up." Horrified, my mum leapt out of her seat to retrieve me from his tiny, loving grip.

We lived at Elliot Close only for a couple of years—the best years. I loved everything about it there. It had a nice family community, with lots of kids for me and Sean to play with. The friendly cul-de-sac felt safe, and the estate, lined with greenery and grassland, made it an ideal place for outdoor adventure. Sean and I and the kids from the neighbourhood would spend hours playing out, using fallen down trees as climbing frames, playing hide and seek in-between the alleyways of the blocks, and chasing one another out into the rolling fields behind the buildings which seemed to go on for miles.

Playing out was the best pastime of all, and at that time in the mid-80s, it felt safe to leave your doors unlocked, or as we did, on the latch and venture out, unattended. Escapades back then only came with two parental caveats—not to go off the estate and not to take sweets from strangers. I personally added a third rule to the list, which bizarrely involved covering my eyes whenever I saw a large black bird.

This was in response to an account I had heard from one of the neighbourhood kids that a woman had her eyes plucked out by a crow. In hindsight, with life experience on my side and my journalistic Spidey senses twitching, I concede that five-year-old me probably could have benefitted from a more in-depth exploration of the fundamental facts of that story, or perhaps should've just run it by an adult.

But at the time, that horrifying information was enough for me to abandon my all-encompassing love for animals and adopt the unusual posture of walking blindly with my hands over my eyes for several paces whenever I saw a large, dark bird. I considered this a small sacrifice in the grand scheme of things, which was essentially keeping my two eyeballs intact!

Elliot Close was also where I met my first crush. He was a year or two older than me and, for all intents and purposes, was considered beyond cool. He had big blue eyes and olive skin, and jet-black hair, with a slick side-parting and a diamanté pierced ear. He lived in our block with his single mum and baby sister. It was one of the few places I could visit without Sean's supervision on account that it didn't involve me leaving the block and the fact that our mums were well acquainted.

It was so fun hanging out at his place because we could play and watch cartoons all day long and his mum was so cool, she let us eat Coco Pops right out of the box with our hands—what more could a kid ask for!

Don't get me wrong, I thought my mum could be cool too, just not 'eat-out-of-the-cereal-box' cool. One area where Mum definitely racked up her cool points was with her car—a sporty white Ford Escort with a spoiler and a thin red racing stripe along the exterior. Even at my young age, I knew that her car was the business, and I would feel sheer exhilaration when she would start up the engine and the twin exhausts and muffler would let out a Formula one hum, commanding the attention of passers-by and fellow motorists alike.

I think that was the first time I thought of my mum as a 'boss'. She was the only woman I knew that drove a sports car. I was proud of it and of her.

However, impressive as it may have been to look at, that's about all you could do with it, because most of the time the darn thing wouldn't start. Most early morning school runs were stifled by the non-compliant empty churning sound of the engine, as it would cough and splutter and refuse to turn over. It became almost standard procedure that whilst Mum would repeatedly turn the key, willing the engine to ignite I would be dismissed from the backseat to go and get help.

Which often consisted of running and buzzing the buzzer of Uncle C and Uncle Yan's place to tell them down the intercom, "Mum's car won't start again!"

Uncle C and Uncle Yan were best friends and lived in the apartment down the hall. Their place was the 'chill-zone', full of bamboo and wicker furniture and the constant sweet and calming aroma of incense and candles filled every room. We loved visiting their place. Sean and I would play dominoes whilst sitting on African print leather pouffes on the floor as Mum, Uncle C and Uncle Yan played vinyls, sipped Guinness punch, and chatted into the evening.

Other times we would visit the Christian family on the ground-floor. They would always greet us with a warm and friendly welcome when we would bump into each other at the building entrance and often invite us over for tea and a bite to eat. They had the ideal playmates for Sean and me—an older daughter plus a boy and a girl our age. I was in such admiration that they had a big sister; she was so pretty and kind. She would let me sit on her lap and let us play games in her room. I was in awe.

Our Elliot Close family brought out the best in us and I loved how Mum was when we lived there. She was happy and content and our home was our haven.

My bedroom at Elliot Close was pretty and colourful and my bedroom accessories were all decorated with Rainbow Brite—an animation princess that was all the rage amongst my peers in the early 80s. Her cartoon show documented her many adventures as she transformed from the character Wisp from a dark and bleak planet into the colourful Rainbow Brite as she collected all the colours of the rainbow and became a 'colour guardian', fending off baddies that sought to steal her spectrum of light. I had the duvet cover, curtain set and wastepaper bin to match—my room was a vibrant, multi-coloured oasis.

Sometimes Sean would let me into his room, and we would play-fight with his Transformer action figures or play music tapes on his tan and chocolate-coloured tape recorder. We would race his toy cars and his big black and grey A-Team truck down the hallway. In his room, we would put our construction skills to the test and attempt to form a bridge from his desk to the bed with a quilt.

In the early days, I always remember us getting along, apart from the time when he discovered I had a phobia of doll's heads being detached from their bodies and popped all the heads of my Sindy dolls off and lined them up outside my bedroom for fun; laughing hysterically whilst I squealed from my room refusing to come out.

I was much more of a solitary child than Sean growing up. Sean was always more sociable. He could move in any circle and behaved much older than his years. Even though he was only around six at the time, the big boys in the neighbourhood would always knock on our front door and plead with my mum to let him play out with them. For as long as I can remember, my brother could make friends with anyone, anywhere.

On a rare family holiday to Butlins, Sean went off to explore by himself and within hours, he returned to our holiday home having made friends with three or four other boys on the resort. I, on the other hand, spent much of the trip blissfully amusing myself and was oblivious to the fear and chaos I had caused when my mum reported me missing whilst I slipped out to the nearby fairground alone and enjoyed several rides on the Mexican Hat, only contemplating my return to our chalet once I had finally run out of fairground tokens.

Sean and I were polar opposites. I was bubbly, outspoken and theatrical yet I enjoyed my solitude—an introverted extrovert—who just loved to escape into her own world where there was boundless space and limitless imagination.

Books were my ultimate escape. I fell in love with the art of storytelling and the vivid imagery it evoked pretty much as soon as I could read. I loved the pictures and would become totally captivated by their artistic detail. I would study the illustrations for minutes at a time, attempting to imprint every detail in my mind before re-reading the passage again, and then attempting to recall to memory with photographic precision the pictures from the previous page.

I submerged myself as I allowed the words to pull me in and tempt me on a new, exciting, fantastical fictional journey. Books ignited my creativity, and I relished the opportunity of opening a brand-new book, inhaling that new book scent and cracking its spine for the first time. Books became my most treasured possession, they were my gateway to another world, my Tardis—transporting me to another realm in another life—and my coveted bookshelf consisted of endless possibilities, taking me wherever and whenever I wanted to go.

Despite the endless opportunities for adventure, my favourite books as a very young child were stories and poems that depicted lead characters who resembled my world or reflected me. I would re-read my favourite titles with such delight, *Amazing Grace* by Mary Hoffman and Caroline Binch, and *Carry, Go, Bring, Come* by Vyanne Samuels and Jennifer Northway over and over; their stories comprising of tales of familial Caribbean delicacies and cultural traditions.

My favourite storybook of all time was *Through My Window* by Tony Bradman and Eileen Browne. The simplistic, yet charming story of a little girl eagerly waiting at the window for the return of her mum from a day's work. The book follows the highs and lows of little Jo's day as she races to and fro from the window, triggered by every resting car engine and squeaky garden gate in the desperate anticipation of her mum's return. Only to be disappointed each time to see it was merely the local postman or friendly milkman coming up the garden path.

I felt a connection to little Jo. She emulated me in so many ways, normally a happy-go-lucky, spirited little girl, who was rendered lost and heartbroken when her mum left to go to work. I shared Jo's feelings of emptiness whilst being left in the care of a guardian or childminder as Mum departed for work and could relate to that feeling of incompleteness that could only be filled by a mother's return. The fact that Jo was also fair-skinned with a curly blondie-brown mane and looked like me only served to further solidify my affinity to her. Spoiler alert—at the end of the book, Jo's mum returns and all happiness is restored.

Books were such a comfort throughout my childhood, and it wasn't long after my introduction to them that I began writing and illustrating stories. Once completed, I would offer an exclusive, intimate reading to my teddy bears and dolls. Lining them up on the bedroom floor, I would sit and read my latest masterpiece aloud. Fine-tuning my storytelling skills, I quickly learnt how to vary my tone and speed to build tension and suspense, incorporating different voices and inflections in my speech to keep my 'captivated' audience entertained.

Turning the pages tantalisingly slowly, I would take my time before revealing my intricate illustrations, designed to accompany and enhance the pleasurable experience for my inanimate listeners. I was in my element.

When I wasn't writing stories or poems, I was making music. If books were my first love, performing was truly my second. I would entertain myself to no end, singing along whilst I composed music on my mini keyboard. I use the term 'composed' loosely because at this point, I could not read music yet and certainly had not mastered the skill of singing in tune yet either!

Other times I would be confined to my room for hours, engrossed in making artistic, creative inventions out of the weird and wonderful things I had collected in my crafts box—cardboard, coloured string, buttons and glitter paint. Mum would occasionally peep into my room to coo and gush over my latest art project or stand laughing in the doorway as I chastised my least favourite doll in one of my self-penned one-woman plays. It wasn't long before Mum signed me up for weekly ballet lessons as a much-needed creative outlet.

Saturday mornings became the highlight of my week, and I was wired from the minute I woke up until we arrived at the dance studio. The excitement would ebb through my body as we arrived, and I could hear the piano playing from the foyer. Brimming with excitement, Mum tried to clothe my excitable, wriggling body in my blush-pink tights and matching leotard for my ballet class, as I would spin in circles like a caged animal trying to break free out of captivity to run unleashed into the wild.

Mum would battle to calm me down and counter my circular motions to successfully tie my baby blue cardigan into a pristine bow, all the while knowing she had a small window to complete what was soon becoming an impossible task, and that as soon as the music stopped, signalling intermission, her time was up. Suddenly, I would make a break for it, bolting towards the dance studio, the anticipation and excitement were impossible for me to contain any longer.

Running as fast as my little legs would take me, I made a dash for it, through the curtained double French doors and away. It was the best rush a five-year-old could hope for.

I don't have many memories of Dad in the early days, but the first memory I do have was on one of those Saturday mornings. Dad was unexpectedly at our flat and despite the abnormality of it all, I was unfazed, bouncing around the place as my mum hurried me to get ready for class and pack my bag. As usual, I was excited and in high spirits.

Ballet class not only meant that I got to dance for an hour, but that I would get to go to Wembley High Street, and that meant I would be allowed to buy a pack of Cola Hubba-Bubba bubble gum from the sweet shop next door before class, and afterwards, I could get a jacket potato from Spudulike on the corner. It was a restaurant franchise that specialised in piping hot baked potatoes and a selection of hot and cold multi-combo fillings—they were delicious, and I always found myself almost salivating as I entered the establishment, excited about my long-anticipated weekend delight!

On this particular morning, Mum was sitting at her dressing table getting ready. Her vanity was adorned with glass bottles of perfumes and creams, make-up, and hair oils, and decorated with an eclectic collection of jewellery and an array of delicate glass animal figurines. The waft of her recently pumped intoxicating Charlie perfume filled the air.

When I entered the room, she had just put on her staple deep magenta lipstick, so I seized the opportunity and asked for a kiss, knowing that some of the purple hue would inevitably transfer onto my nude lips. Mwah!

I ran to the hallway mirror and examined my new look, thrilled I returned to the room excited to show my dad my instant makeover. Unimpressed and with little acknowledgement, he told me to hand him a tissue, and as soon as I passed it to him, he wiped the lipstick clean off my lips and turned away. As I left the flat with Mum, I was silent, overwhelmed with a rush of emotions.

I was in complete shock. I kept replaying the recent event over and over in my head as Mum and I rode in the car to class. My disappointment was deeper than my smudged lips. It wasn't about the lipstick at all in fact. He had ruined my moment and broken my trust; it was an act of betrayal—*how could he?*

This was my first awakening.

2

Forbidden Fruit

Mum and Dad met in the 70s as teenagers, and were high school sweethearts; although technically, they didn't officially begin dating until after they had finished their O-levels (that's GCSEs to all the millennials).

They began their courtship at a time when aeroplane shirt colours and bell bottoms were in fashion and anyone that was anyone in their friendship group donned the biggest honorary Jackson 5 afro they could possibly pluck!

I always compare Mum and Dad's love story to that of Sandy Olsson and Danny Zuko from the musical *Grease*. They were complete opposites—Mum was the shy, unassuming, church girl and Dad was the popular, sporty, rule-breaking maverick.

Mum was raised in a strict Christian household. Her parents emigrated to the UK from Barbados in the late 50s. She was the seventh of eight siblings and the first to be born in England, which at times, alienated her from her older siblings who thought she had it too easy this side of the pond. Friends would often marvel at the fact that she came from such a big family, but Mum would often lament that at times she felt like she didn't have four older brothers but in fact had five fathers due to her stringent home life.

My mum's parents came from humble beginnings but worked hard and bought their home in a cul-de-sac on the outskirts of Kensal Green, where they would go on to live out their lives. It was a typical Caribbean home—the walls were adorned with staple velvet cloth maps depicting their home island, each parish separated by colourful silk thread and listed by name. They had an impeccable front room, only to be frequented by the most esteemed guests, complete with a glass cabinet and drinks trolley, scrolls with parables and Bible scriptures and the serenity prayer decorating the interior.

Granny, Mum's Mum, worked as a school cook, and mealtimes at home were often a fusion of Bajan delicacies and hearty English traditions. Grandad S was a heating engineer—a responsible, conscientious worker and devoted royalist—who was honoured to receive Her Majesty's award of an Imperial Service medal for his committed long service. Usually an unassuming and discreet man, he was delighted to have his photo taken to accompany his badge of honour for the local paper.

As devout Christians, the entire family attended church several times a week and were active members. Granny was always on hand to help out in the church kitchen and led praise and worship unofficially from the pews! Grandad was a church deacon, on account of his reliability and responsible nature. He was dependable and generous and everyone at church knew that they could rely on him in a crisis.

He would routinely make multiple trips on a Sunday morning before and after church service, ferrying fellow members of the congregation back and forth to their homes in his little navy-blue Cavalier hatchback.

Mum's homelife growing up was routine, structured and disciplined. As a teenager, she was determined to break out of the rigid, conventional blueprint that had been pre-determined for her. She was a free thinker; she craved freedom; she didn't want tradition; she wanted something different… cue my dad.

Dad's lifestyle represented everything that Mum's domesticity did not. He was the oldest of four children, born in England to Jamaican immigrant parents. Young parents themselves. In the early years, Grandad M worked as a presser and a tailor and my nan was a chambermaid. When Dad was born, Nan gave up work to stay at home and raise him and his consequent siblings. Grandad M continued to work and support the family, groundbreakingly starting his own dry-cleaning business in the 80s.

My dad's freedom eclipsed that of my mum's. He didn't have a curfew, there were fewer house rules to abide by, and money was less tight. My mum was in awe of the autonomy my dad exhibited—coming and going as he pleased, having friends over whenever he wanted, partaking in after-school activities and attending weekend dances. Dad's world intrigued her, it was exciting and thrilling, and most importantly, was lightyears away from her own, just what she wanted.

I think Mum and Dad were equally attracted to each other but for completely different reasons; Mum was drawn to the freedom and free-spiritedness of my dad. He wasn't a wild child per se, but he was carefree and unrestrained, not afraid to break the rules and push the boundaries. He was uninhibited and fun; he took risks and didn't worry about the consequences. He broadened her horizons and offered her a means to break out of the mould.

In turn, I think my dad was drawn to my mum's innocence and naivety. She was sensitive and sentimental, kind and considerate. She had good, wholesome values and represented 'wifey' material. I think he was attracted to her family dynamic, and maybe deep down in his boundless world, that was something he craved and wanted—a tight-knit family of his own.

At 19, they began planning to have a child. My dad was adamant that he wanted to be a young dad just like his dad was, and so he made his parents grandparents at 40. My nan was overjoyed and idolised my brother.

My mum's side of the family were less pleased and struggled to hide their disapproval and disappointment, which translated in my mum's eyes as judgement and condemnation, which ultimately drove a wedge between them. And so, when the opportunity arose for her young family to be housed in a flat on the other side of London, she took it. Deep down, my mum knew her family loved her, but she was unmarried, with a baby, this was the opposite of everything her upbringing should've taught her.

At school, Mum had always been academically very bright. Music and English were her favourite lessons besides drama. She was a talented performer and landed lead roles in most of the school plays and musicals. Shy and lacking in confidence, she came into her own when she was performing on stage. When she was acting and singing, she was able to put all her niggling insecurities to the back of her mind, as she and her character became one. Being on stage gave her a rush and a newfound confidence.

Mum and Dad went around in a big co-ed group at school. But Mum says she always felt like the outcast, often the target of religious jibes or left out by members of the group that had more lenient parental controls. My dad, on the other hand, was a popular kid. Every bit the jock, bright but not necessarily academically inspired, he was a football fanatic, convinced that he would go pro one day. He was a hit with the guys and the girls, who were charmed by his confidence and charisma.

After high school, Mum stayed on and completed her A-Levels. Soon after, she landed herself a prestigious job as a court clerk. Dad was training to be an electrician when he dropped out of college and for a while worked as an assistant on a market stall. He was much better suited to the non-academic life and took to the early mornings and the market trader culture naturally.

But it was not all a bed of roses; barely adults themselves, they were now on their own, fending for themselves, in a town they didn't know, isolated from family and friends, raising a child. They would infrequently visit relatives and occasionally family would visit them in their two-bedroom flat in Catford, but relationships with parents and their siblings were strained, and communication was often tense.

At 21, Mum and Dad planned for another child and not long after, I came along. It was a second blow for the family. And then when I was four years old, Mum and Dad did the unthinkable, and eloped! The taboo act remained concealed from many family members until one year later, at their wedding blessing.

The ceremony a year after their nuptials was an elaborate affair. On a sunny day in June, Mum and Dad reaffirmed their vows to one another in an extravagant church in the Hampshire countryside, in front of a bridal party of 12 and more than 200 guests.

A flashy parade of vintage Rolls Royce for the bride, bridesmaids, flower girls and page boys, and my dad and his groomsmen arrived in a sports car convoy with Dad's Porsche at the helm. It was a statement wedding and an act of victory over the doubters. This ceremony was not just about their commitment to one another, but it was a message to 'the establishment'. They had proved the naysayers wrong and the whole event said nothing short of 'Look at us now, we've made it!'.

This day wasn't just Mum and Dad's, they made it about all four of us. We went out as a strong, united family unit, and looked every bit the part as we posed and smiled for photos. I felt like a princess, my hair pressed and coiffured by a professional hairstylist. I was adorned in a pearl jewellery set, complete with a necklace and droplet earrings. I wore a peach puff-ball bridesmaid dress, lace cream fingerless gloves and silk ballet pumps.

I took on the secret challenge with the other flower girls of seeing who could lower their bardot dress the furthest without being detected by an adult. We collectively declared our mission successful when we posed for our bridal party photos with the neckline of our dresses inches below our armpits!

Sean and the other page boys were turned out handsomely in their three-piece, cream silk suits complete with bowties and razor-sharp fades (haircuts).

As we left for the church that morning, all the page boys and flower girls began piling into the classic fleet of cars parked lining the street, but as I followed suit, Mum called me back.

"Nicola, you aren't going with them," she said. "You and Sean are coming with me in my car!" My mouth dropped open in utter disappointment. I burst into tears as I turned my back towards her, arms folded, pouting, staring at Mum's black Golf GTI parked on the kerbside.

I turned back towards her only to protest, "I don't want to go in your car!" before defiantly turning away for the ultimate diva-effect, when my mum let out an unexpected roar of laughter.

"Not my car silly, *my* car—that's my car!" She replied. As I turned reluctantly, following the direction of her pointed finger, the most magnificent Rolls Royce came into view, more exquisite than the others, adorned with an ivory bow. "That's my car," she said.

It was glorious. And in one instance, my frown immediately faded and was replaced by a genial grin. Wasting no time, I ran over to the door being held open by a chauffeur, clambered into the back seat of the cream-lined cab and sat up, brimming with excitement. As we pulled off, waving to friends and neighbours who had lined the street to witness the spectacle, I felt like royalty. As we turned the corner, Mum leant down to me and jibed, "Silly Billy."

I chuckled, relieved, wiping the remnants of tears from my face with the back of my hand. I sat back and looked out of the window and sighed, all was restored. It was going to be a perfect day.

Posing for pics with her parents before the ceremony, Mum was more than just executing traditional customs, this act was symbolic and told them she wanted them to be involved, not just today but for the future and in all of our lives. And her parents' presence and willingness to smile and participate was just the reciprocation of the olive branch she needed. It was a gesture of support and signalled a truce; a hope for a new beginning and a fresh start.

So, there it was, Mum finally had her fairy tale. She was about to walk down the aisle and enter her new life, this time with the love of her life, her children and her family all by her side. So how could she possibly bring herself to tell anyone, especially her family that it was all a facade and that her happily ever after was already falling apart?

It was at the 'big house', that I first remember us living together as a family. The big house was our semi-detached, double fronted home in the suburbs of South Kenton.

To the outside world, the land and blueprint of our home was beyond impressive—double car garage, through lounge, French patio doors that opened out on to a 100-foot garden, complete with blackberry trees and outdoor brick barbecue area. To the unassuming eye, it looked like a dream home, but inside it was a shambles. We knew how it looked outwardly, but make no mistake, Sean and I knew better than most, that we were not even close to keeping up with the Joneses and that by all accounts we were poor—despite our impressive postcode.

The internal walls of the house were bare, the colour of plaster and cement. There was no carpet in any of the rooms apart from the lounge, and remnants of underlay covered parts of the floorboards in places where it hadn't worn away. The kitchen was missing an entire wall and directly opened out into the garage, making it cold and draughty. The wooden table in the kitchen against the adjoining wall doubled up as a storage area for our sundries and crockery.

One bedroom was uninhabitable due to it being damp and poorly insulated; so, for the first time Sean and I shared a room, which was a catastrophe waiting to happen.

I hated living in the big house. It was a world away from the cosy confines of our flat in Elliot Close. My parents argued all the time. Mum wanted to pool the family finances in efforts to make the shell of our house more of a home, whilst Dad focused all his efforts and funds on his bodybuilding and starting his video business which he ran out of the converted garage.

Once enthralled by his lax, open-door policy at his childhood home, Mum now resented coming home from work and finding his friends and staff hanging out in the lounge and helping themselves to food in the fridge. Dad felt unsupported in his dreams and ambition and that Mum was being short-sighted towards his vision by insisting they focus on their present living conditions and felt that an initial sacrifice would pay dividends in the long run. Meanwhile, Mum wanted financial stability and to be able to stop living hand to mouth; as a result, the house was a warzone.

Soon after moving to the big house, Sean and I changed schools and began attending a school in an affluent, tight-knit community. The school was on impressive grounds, had great academic and music facilities, but was every bit institutionally racist.

I missed my old school where I didn't have to wear a uniform, where the teachers were nice, and where I could see my best friend, Peter. I missed my beloved Cath, our former chain-smoking, rough-around-the-edges, fun-loving childminder.

Cath had the deepest, huskiest voice I had ever heard on a woman, that would erupt into violent fits of coughing and spluttering whenever she let out a hearty laugh, which was often. She was probably not the most PC custodian, but boy did she love us! She lived on a council estate in North Wembley and Sean, and I loved playing out with the neighbourhood kids and the other children she cared for.

She had fun toys and games for us to play with as we entertained ourselves for hours on the kitchen floor whilst she pottered around stepping over us as she fixed us snacks and made our 'tea', stopping occasionally to engage with cartoons we were watching on the TV affixed to the wall or to teach us about the meals she was preparing and introducing us to new, funny sounding words like 'petits pois'.

But now we were living in a snooty part of town and had to call our childminders aunty and uncle. We were picked up in a black cab every day and taken to their detached house where they would throw toast and jam to us and the other kids like it was feeding time at the zoo. The house was brimming with children; it was utter chaos and I doubt in all the time they looked after us if they even knew our names.

In the evenings, Dad would watch us. When business was slow, he and his delivery drivers would hang out in the living room, working out or watching movies, sometimes women would come over too. When Mum was home from work, they were always fighting. I would run into my bedroom and climb under the covers to muffle the sound of raised voices and the smashing and crashing of inanimate objects breaking against walls.

After an altercation, Dad would always leave, and I would emerge from my hiding place often to find Mum fighting back tears as she swept up broken glass and attempted to clean up all evidence of the destruction that had just ripped through the house like a merciless tornado.

On one occasion, recognising the audible pattern of shouting and threats followed by the all too familiar sound of Dad's footsteps nearing the front door, I pounced from my bedroom to protest his imminent departure. Sobbing through pleas from the top of the stairs as he moved towards the front door, he stopped in his tracks in shock and for a moment stood dumbfounded, glancing up at me at the top of the stairwell before hardheartedly turning to my mum and saying, "Your daughter's crying!" before walking through the door and slamming it behind him.

The screeching sound of his car tyres followed in quick succession as he pulled out of the driveway and hurtled towards the end of the road and off into the distance.

Devastated, I stayed glued to the spot as Mum climbed the stairs and attempted to console me. I didn't understand how he could abandon me. I didn't understand why he didn't stay, especially for me.

For as long as I can remember, I had always idolised my dad. We had a special bond that we couldn't explain, but both felt in equal measure. I had always gravitated towards him. He was the only one to ever tell me emphatically that he loved me. I knew Mum loved me too, but he and I spoke the same 'language'. He was passionate with his words; he just got me and all my quirks like no one else did.

He was able to make me feel special just by being in his presence. He would call me endearing nicknames and showing affection towards me came naturally to him in a way that it didn't with me and Mum. Dad and I bonded whilst he taught me how to shave his beard, how to tie a tie, how to polish my school shoes, and how to make the best homemade hot chocolate—chocolate powder first, then the milk, then the sugar, then the hot water—it was a game changer!

If I had a nightmare in the middle of the night, I would sneak into my parents' bedroom, walk all the way around the bed and climb in and curl up behind him. He was my safe place. I mimicked everything he did, even putting my t-shirts on like him—arms first and then the head. It definitely wasn't a practical way to put on my apparel, but if Dad did it, it was good enough for me.

But now he was gone, and I couldn't reconcile what had just happened. I couldn't comprehend that he had just abandoned me and once again had broken my trust.

Within a few days, he returned, but the damage was done, and my anxiety only heightened every time he left, that this time would be the last time and that one day, he would leave and never return.

The dysfunctionality in our family spread like a disease, and Sean and I, once inseparable, became arch-enemies, and now fought over everything. He was no longer my protector, and I was no longer his 'little sister'. It was nothing like it was at Elliot Close. It was as if now that we lived with Dad in the big house, Sean had lost his fatherly role and now it was more like every man for himself.

My dad was complex. He had an all-consuming personality which made him infectious and thrilling to be around at times. He was the 'fun' parent and a prankster. I definitely learnt charm and wit from him. He would teach us naughty jokes and give us cryptic riddles to work out. But there was another side to him.

On the flip side, he was a staunch disciplinarian, with a violent temper. Towering over us at an impressive six-foot and four-inches tall his unpredictable temperament meant that in his presence you were always on high alert and were abundantly aware of the fact that things could swiftly change in the blink of an eye. He knowingly ruled our home with an iron fist, capitalising on our fear of him—the psychological mistreatment often worse than the physical.

One day whilst Mum was at work and I was watching cartoons in the living room, he summoned me into his office to let me know that he was aware that my brother and I had used swear words during an argument with one another. He then presented me with a gut-wrenching ultimatum, fess up in 30 minutes who the instigator was or we'd both get a spanking. He then dismissed me back to the living room to resume watching my cartoons and to watch the clock.

Despite how hard I tried, I couldn't possibly re-immerse myself back into the eventful plotline of Pink Panther with this big black cloud now looming overhead. 30 minutes felt like an eternity and this dilemma was too much for my six-year-old brain to comprehend. Before the half an hour was up, I had gone back into his office and was virtually pleading with him to do it and get it over with.

Like two bulls in a pen, Dad seemed to make light entertainment for himself out of pitting Sean and I against each other and enticing us to compete for everything, including poll position as his favourite child. Everything was a contest: who could win a race, who could win a taste test, who could run an errand and get everything on the list, who would fail and return empty-handed, who was the smartest, and who got to sit in the front seat of his Porsche, or delivery van?

I didn't know it then but the sibling rivalry that he ignited would come at a price and the damage it would cause to the relationship between my brother and I would be virtually irreversible for years to come.

To make matters worse, Sean and I didn't have neighbourhood friends anymore. The families on our street kept to themselves. The neighbour to the left of us was an unfriendly, single, middle-aged man, who had an overgrown, uninviting front garden and a car blocking his front door. He was so hostile and intimidating that Sean and I would 'ip-dip' every time one of us had to knock on his door and ask to retrieve our ball from his back garden. His space outback soon became our toy graveyard.

Our neighbours on the right-hand-side were really welcoming. Their household consisted of three generations, and they were a tight-knit family—cooking together, having mealtimes together and hanging out in the garden as a group. From our garden, I would look on and admire their harmonious dynamic and unwavering closeness, they were so lucky I thought.

The grandma, the matriarch of the family, would often pop her head over the fence and invite me over to join them for dinner. She made an amazing vegetable curry and my favourite—chapatis. Sean was a fussy eater and often declined, but I never turned down a meal!

They were kind and generous neighbours and Sean, and I loved playing on their huge climbing frame erected in their backyard, especially when our garden became so overgrown that it wasn't fun to play in anymore.

Other than infrequent visits next door, the only outside time we did get was when we would occasionally ride our bikes or skate to the shops on errands for Dad. Sometimes, he would let us keep his change and we would buy penny sweets and a bottle of pop from the corner shop. Other times, he would send us to mail his business leaflets in the neighbourhood, after school and on the weekends, whilst Mum was at work.

We would jump at the chance, delighting in the opportunity to get out and explore the area, often deviating from our instructed route and taking a little longer than permitted to return, which often landed us in trouble.

It wasn't all bad at the big house. There were the odd occasions when Mum and Dad would get along and they would treat us to a Chinese takeaway with all the trimmings—prawn balls, King Prawn chow mein, egg fried rice and fried beef in black bean sauce. Dad would get the crab soup for starters, and on occasion, he would let me have a few sips.

It was on those odd occasions that I would see Mum and Dad's playful and competitive sides as they selected board games for the evening's entertainment and battled against one another during an intense game of Trivial Pursuit or Scrabble, as I inserted myself as quiz master or tile juggler. It was in these blissful, infrequent moments that we felt like a proper family.

Dad would teach Sean how to play chess on his electronic chessboard and there was one famous game of Battleship they played that after an hour of no sunken ships, Mum in disbelief coerced a double-sided confession, which left us all in fits of laughter as they fessed up that they had both been cheating and strategically moving their ships to avoid annihilation!

We went to theme parks as a family too and as soon as we were tall enough for the big rides, we went on them all. More Dad's passion than Mum's, due to her motion sickness. Nonetheless, she was a trooper and went along anyway. Sean and I would scream as we hurtled down the log flume or on the Black Hole ride, encouraged by our adrenaline-driven dad to put our hands in the air at the scariest parts to maximise the thrill of the experience.

Sean and I obliged, with mouths wide open and eyes tightly shut, our fear masked in funny expressions, captured by an opportune paparazzi flash at the climax of the ride, memorialised in a photo frame which Mum and Dad purchased from the souvenir shop for future endless amusement. Other photos depicted us drenched from head to toe after going on the toboggan ride and unassumingly sitting in the seats allocated by Dad, which we would later discover were shrewdly selected by him for our optimum drenching.

Emerging from the ride, our plastic overalls were sodden wet, proving their inadequacy in effectively keeping our attire beneath dry, Dad would be in hysterics. But we didn't mind, it was all in fun. The main thing was everyone was happy, for once. In those moments, I wished we could have just frozen in time forever.

But it wasn't long before the seas would change and back home, the laughter and frolicking of days past felt like a distant memory as the arguing escalated and the fighting ensued. When Mum and Dad eventually separated, we moved in with her parents, Granny and Grandad S. Sean and I had our own rooms again and we had a whole neighbourhood full of our childhood friends to play out with that we usually only saw on the weekends. Everything seemed so much better there, and we weren't missing our life at the big house at all.

Living with Granny and Grandad S brought about an unexplainable peace, and once again, our home felt like exactly that, a home, physically and emotionally. We loved it there and we could tell Granny and Grandad S liked having us there too. The typical generational gripes of being told off for unintentionally slamming doors or being reprimanded for running up and down the stairs didn't seem to faze us and were inconsequential in the grand scheme of our domestic bliss.

We went to church with Granny and Grandad S every Sunday, whilst Mum worked one of her many jobs. They were strict guardians, but we always knew they loved us. We knew they weren't rich but somehow, we never seemed to go without. I guess Granny's resourcefulness in raising eight children somehow enabled her to always ensure that there was enough to go around.

She would regularly give us money to buy ice cream and sweets if we asked. Ushering us to go and get her purse was the celebratory signal we needed to confirm our requests had been approved and that sweet relief was imminent.

Not a week went by when Granny wasn't baking and icing her latest sweet treats. I was often close by waiting in the wings for the cue as sous-chef, that it was my turn to help with the whisking machine before retreating to the kitchen table where I was granted the rare privilege of licking the spoon and consuming all surplus sweet batter mix.

Granny was like Mum in the kitchen, bossy and impatient with anyone who got in her way or under her feet. That also included asking persistent questions about when her latest creation would be ready out of the oven or trying to pin her down on specific quantities and recipe methodology that she clearly only kept in her head. In all the years I observed her, I don't ever recall seeing her meticulously reading a recipe or following cooking instructions (although I'm told she did) either way, her cakes never failed.

They were always the right balance of sweetness and fluffiness, and the only complaint she ever received was that with an extended family of almost 30, they were always gone way too quickly.

When she wasn't in the kitchen, Granny loved to watch TV. During the week, she would watch her staple soaps—*Neighbours, Home and Away, Coronation Street* and *Brookside*. In the early afternoon, she'd watch her quiz shows—*Fifteen to One, Blockbusters* and *Countdown*, and at the weekend, it was all about the gameshows—*Blankety Blank, Bullseye* and *Catchphrase*. Saturday evenings were reserved for a classic crime thriller movie which would split either side of the ten o'clock news.

It was always at the most gripping, climatic part that we would be interrupted by Trevor McDonald to give us the latest news from the ITN studios. When the film resumed and the plot would continue to unfold, Granny would yell unceremoniously at the screen as the damsel in distress proceeded down a dimly lit alley or to enter a sinister-looking building. We would laugh and snigger beside her on the sofa as she would scold them aloud for not heeding her warning, as the story climaxed, and the main character arrived in a predicament spelling untold disaster.

Watching TV in our family was a bonding experience, and almost a learnt expression of love, enjoying one another and spending time together.

On sick days from school, Granny would bundle me up on the sofa, swaddled in my favourite pink floral blanket, with my feet tucked behind her back whilst she perused the telly book for our next televisual delight. During my college days, I would return during free periods to reunite, and watch *Murder She Wrote* or *Columbo*, and chime in as we would shout out our suspicious peppered cries of 'He's guilty' or 'She done it!' at the screen.

Grandad S, on the other hand, was all about the Westerns, and I enjoyed watching them with him on Saturday afternoons, seated next to him, back against the sofa on the carpeted floor, we would watch the likes of *Rawhide* or anything featuring Clint Eastwood in the line-up.

At bedtime, he would tell us ghost stories and chase us around the house playing the Frankenstein monster game as we would squeal and run up the stairs—a designated area of relief from the scary character who could not ascend to such great heights (less monster related, more likely related to the fact that Grandad S was in his late 60s).

The game would pause while we would grow increasingly bored with our newfound safety in the upper confinements of the house, before daring to venture back downstairs to seek out the whereabouts of the 'scary man', only to return seconds later shrieking with excitement as he re-emerged, hot on our heels.

It was at Granny and Grandad S's that I taught myself how to play the piano. A once forbidden front room during my mum's childhood was now accessible, free of rules and regulations for us. I spent hours in there, learning the notes, and then the scales, and then eventually delving into Granny's music books to teach myself how to play songs and melodies. Occasionally, I would slide back the big glass door partition and beckon Mum or Granny in for guidance, relying on their musically trained ears for help.

But only when it was completely perfected and polished, and I had practised countless times without error, would I invite them in to perform a mini recital.

About the only thing Granny and Grandad S didn't embrace about me was my love for animals. I would constantly coax the neighbour's cats into the back garden to play, sneaking them out bowls of water and tempting them with pieces of string. I would be fascinated by woodlice and collect snails I found by the shed. Grandad S especially did not approve, and I was convinced his modus operandi was to be the ultimate saboteur.

Whenever I was presenting my imaginary wildlife show in the backyard, he'd come out from the house, shouting and waving his spade in the air, scaring all my bug-friends away. Therefore, it is testament to their loving and generous natures that they ever agreed to allow me to keep my pet hamster at their home, which in their eyes was basically a rat in a cage!

Granny and Grandad S's house felt safe, it was a place of happiness and togetherness. Undoubtedly, the best time of all was Boxing Day. It was our annual tradition for the entire extended family to get together the day after Christmas to celebrate. Every family member from all over London earmarked that day in their calendar knowing that come 26 December, all roads lead to NW10.

Granny loved the holidays, especially Christmas and she relished the opportunity to finally have the tree brought down from the loft and to put up her festive decorations. The walls and ceilings were draped with reams of multi-coloured, chintzy bunting, organised with no real colour-scheme or pattern of design, just the collaborative effort of my granny and her decorators to ensure that not one inch of wallpaper was left bare.

The sweet aroma of cinnamon spice, coconut and nutmeg wafted from the kitchen and invaded every room on the ground-floor. In the grand front room, the Christmas tree towered above a heaped pile of presents, overflowing, the array of vibrantly wrapped gifts occupied every inch of the carpet under the leafy canopy.

Every few minutes, the front door would open followed by the *tring* of the doorbell. This was also a tradition of ours. The ring was two-fold; it alerted the occupants inside the house that a visitor was at the door, but the light inflection of the chime signalled a familial presence that conveyed the universally understood message 'Don't worry, it's only *me*, letting myself in!'

Hugs and what felt like a hundred hellos would follow before the next carload of family members would arrive in quick succession and we would repeat the ritual all over again, until all were present and accounted for, and every room was brimming with people and the soundtrack of spirited conversation and laughter played out throughout the house.

Each new guest would eventually divert their attention in the direction of the kitchen in hopes of a preview and potentially a sample of Granny's baked spoils. Leading her guests to the kitchen down the hallway, enroute she would joke and tease that she hadn't had time to make their favourite dishes or that the food had miraculously already run out.

Unperturbed by her jesting, they would proceed, eager in anticipation and enter in, only to discover a spread fit for a king—coconut bread, pudding, black cake, bread pudding and homemade mince pies, and that was just the sweet treats! There was smoked ham stuffed with cloves, turkey, stuffing, gungo peas and rice, home-made coleslaw, beetroot, plain cucumber for the faint-hearted and spicy pickled cucumber with Bajan pepper sauce for the more fearless palettes.

After dinner, we would watch telly and graze from the dining table of temptation, often venturing out to the kitchen for the overflow of snacks and titbits that had been unable to fit and be showcased on the main table alongside the elaborate dining assortment of delectable treats. Once we were all officially stuffed, it was time for presents.

It was family custom that we would all congregate around the tree and the youngest of the grandchildren would do the honours in reading out each gift tag before delivering it into the hands of its rightful owner. This tradition often served the youngsters well as the present pile was often skewed in their favour.

Anticipation grew as everyone sat and waited patiently as each gift was announced and the gift giver was thanked before the gift was passed onto its eagerly awaiting recipient. Then we all opened our gifts at the same time. After present time, it was time for games; Monopoly, Ludo and Uno. Playing games was no quiet affair in our family, despite frequent ssh-ing and calls for overexcited relatives to calm down; the noise only intermittently died down before it escalated again.

Playfully, we would argue about the same things every year which would always result in petitions to revisit the rule book, after someone attempted to play a Draw Four card on top of a Draw Two or conduct a forbidden step like adding a Skip on top of a Reverse card. Those protesting the loudest usually being the challenger along with the subsequent players who principally benefitted from the controversial move.

The game soon became abandoned as the room erupted with fits of laughter as Grandad S unknowingly revealed his entire hand as he quizzed his opponents as to whether the card, he was about to play was blue or green!

3
Justice vs Just Is

Perhaps it's the Libra in me that has caused me to always seek out balance and equality, but even as a child, I was passionate about it, and if I experienced or witnessed any injustice, it would deeply affect me and ignite within me an unshakeable compulsion to want to right the wrong. Adults often categorised my response as a child as being too sensitive or having an inability to let things go, but it was deeper than that.

A usually bubbly, happy, outgoing child, I would become paralysed and consumed by the unfair treatment of myself or someone else, and the desire to restore the balance would be overwhelming. It was more than an urge, it almost felt innate, and I simply couldn't bear to just stand by and do nothing.

Naturally outspoken and confident, I was not a confrontational child. But there was something about wrongdoings that propelled me to override all my natural instincts and insecurities and speak up. Perhaps it was the essence behind my name, which translated from Greek literally means 'Victory of the people'. Maybe the power of my name gave me some divine calling.

But whatever it was, I just couldn't shake it. As a child, I was never quite able to put my finger on what that burning desire within me was, but as an adult, I have come to affectionately call it my Rosa Parks spirit!

I was soon to learn that this act of putting my head above the parapet and speaking up would come at a price, that would often be to my detriment. My first experience was at primary school at the age of six, where I was subjected to physical and verbal assaults by the boys in my class and leisure time outside of the classroom was frequently littered with inflicted kicks, punches and racial slurs.

However, despite the daily taunts and frequent assaults, any time one of my friends would suffer an injustice by one of the boys, I would feel compelled to intervene and take it upon myself to retrieve their stolen ball or insist my pal be issued an apology for being knocked over during their reckless play. As a result, I became enemy number one. I would often spend playtime unsuccessfully trying to avoid being detected by their radar and being blasted in the face by their football as they used me for target practice.

When they seemingly couldn't get a reaction from me, they would confront me head on, and after a few choice words, it always escalated to a well-coordinated attack. I did my best to defend myself which often resulted in me being outnumbered in a tussle with the main instigators of the group, delivering jabs and thrusts, from the fringes of the group as I fought back. All the while praying that a teacher's whistle was imminent, to extract me and disperse my bullies.

It felt like the cavalry had finally arrived and a gush of relief swept over me as the short sharp pip-pip-pip sound pierced the air and grew louder. My shirt and tie dishevelled, my hair in disarray, and cheeks flushed bright pink, I was plucked from the ground. I examined my cuts and scrapes and fought back tears as I and my 'opponent' were marched to the headteacher's office.

Wherever possible, I relied on my words rather than my brawn, to defend myself against my tormentors and got impressively skilled at it. One day in class, one boy shouted towards me, "Hey, plunger mouth!"

Another scoffed. "Her lips are so big they look like they are made of rubber!"

A third shouted, "Yeah, we should call her rubber lips!"

Masking my embarrassment, I turned to the most recent heckler and said, "And we should call your dad *just for men* because first his hair was grey and now it's black!" (A quip relating to the popular hair dying brand in the 80s that took a silver fox to dark and debonair all in the space of one wash, or at least according to the advertising campaign).

A gradual hush filled the room as my retort silenced my enemies and I let out a subtle sigh of relief, allowing myself to enjoy the brief respite, knowing only too well I would soon pay the price for my rebuttal.

It was breaktime and I was skipping with friends in the playground when a group of five or six of the usual suspects in my class formed a coordinated semi-circle around me. My heart began racing as I realised my 'payback' was imminent. I tried to stand my ground, fixing my facial expression to seemingly appear unperturbed, as I braced myself for whatever fresh hell they were about to unleash, when by surprise and out of my peripheral view, the boy I had confronted earlier in class, ran at me full speed from behind, stabbing me sharply with his elbow in my back.

I fell to the ground, winded and fighting to breathe. As I clambered to my feet, I locked eyes with the teacher on duty, her mouth fell open, her expression of shock and disbelief, instantly conveyed that she had seen the whole thing. With tears streaming down my face and knees bleeding and bruised, I painfully brushed my stinging palms which were now embedded with stones from the asphalt that had broken my fall.

Amidst tears and emotional stutters, I ran towards the teacher, gasping for air as I tried to verbalise my complaint. I had only managed to get out a few words when she cut me off with her emotionless tone. "Well, stay away from them then!" She said, before turning her back and walking away in the opposite direction.

For the first time, my heart felt the sharp pang of injustice. This was my second awakening.

I don't know if I knew before junior school that I was Black. Maybe I did on some subconscious level, I really can't be sure, but what I am certain of is that it was at junior school, that I first learnt that it mattered.

I didn't like it in junior school. I missed my infant class 2K and my favourite teacher Miss Kittow. She would've protected me. Miss Kittow was not like the other teachers at school. She was kind and fun and unconventional. She was from New Zealand and would teach us all about the indigenous Māori people during 'carpet time'. She taught us how to weave leaves and make piu piu skirts and brought in native instruments and staple foods from her fascinating culture.

2K were the envy of the whole school and pupils from other classes would hover enviously at the doorway of her classroom during extended toilet breaks, just to catch a glimpse of what exciting entertainment Miss Kittow had to bestow on her lucky pupils that day.

She once had a mobile kitchen wheeled into our classroom one afternoon and proceeded to cook us tasty treats from her captivating homeland. The delightful aroma wafted down the hallway and soon drew the attention of teachers in neighbouring classrooms, who began to congregate at the classroom entrance, eager to get a sample of her native culinary delights.

I loved Miss Kittow and she loved me. There was always a sparkle in her eye, and she knew just how to make every child feel uniquely special. Mum was convinced I was Miss Kittow's favourite, her view reinforced as I gleefully recapped my day at the dining table and told of how Miss Kittow had selected me as class monitor whilst she had briefly stepped out or had chosen me as her assistant for a class demonstration.

At parent's evening, Mum would affectionately warn her not to overindulge me or give me special treatment, but she would just shrug and smile and warmly reply, "It's no problem!"

But now Miss Kittow was gone, and junior school had catapulted me from the safe security of the paddling pool into the choppy, relentless waves of the big, blue ocean, without a life jacket in sight.

In the classroom is where I felt most safe. It is where I could sit apart from my bullies and immerse myself in learning, which I loved. English comprehension was my favourite subject. I thoroughly enjoyed the exercises; filling in blanks with a word or phrase from the multiple-choice options suspended in a bubble at the bottom of the page or guessing the definition of a list of innocuous words listed down the right-hand side of the textbook.

Attending an affluent school had a few perks, and I found light relief participating in a range of academic and extracurricular activities—origami class, book club, music recording sessions and swimming lessons in the outdoor swimming pool.

Once a week, we had handwriting lessons with a cursive teacher. Learning how to put loops and strokes on the beginnings and ends of our letters was enjoyable for an academic nerd like me. Coupled with the exciting prospect of being upgraded to Berol ballpoint and then on to Fountain pen, once the technique had been perfected beyond critique, was all the encouragement I needed.

I relished the challenge and became a perfectionist, practising and practising until I could create identical letters on every line and seamlessly join them up. Totally unfazed by the all too familiar permanent blue ink smudge on my outer left hand as my uncommon writing hand unavoidably tracked across the page.

In art class, I would sneakily take two sheets of paper when they were handed out, one for practice and one for the finished article. There was nothing worse I surmised than creating a masterpiece only to detect the faint lines and rubbings out of earlier misgivings. I wanted it to be perfect, whatever it was. I get that trait from my dad, watching him draw sketches and trace characters from my storybooks with immaculate precision.

Every one of my artistic creations had to, in my eyes, be of an exceptional standard—all the shading had to go in the same direction and absolutely none of the colouring-in could deviate outside of the lines. It had to be as perfect as Dad's.

Another skill I was determined to perfect was my pop-up art, after we were taught how to make pop-up books one day in class. I found it fascinating and was determined to master the technique until I had it down pat and was overjoyed when the teacher set the class the task of applying what we had learnt to make our very own pop-up books. I was raring to go. My experience and love for storybooks put me on notice that it wasn't just about the illustrations but that the storyline had to be equally as engaging.

After some deep thought, I came up with the elaborate narrative which consisted of a boxing match between two imaginary arch-rival characters; Cecil, the Centipede—heroin and 'underdog' (for want of a better expression) and the villain, Simon, the Spider. They would duke it out in a ring-side competition to win the affection of Lucy, the Ladybird.

I was so engrossed in my work of art that when the teacher dismissed the class for break time and proceeded to leave the room, I barely even noticed. As my classmates flew out of the room and exploded out onto the playground outside, screaming and squealing, excited about their brief hiatus, I successfully pleaded with her to allow me to stay indoors and complete my creation.

Twenty minutes later, when the bell rang signalling the end of break and the class filed back into the room, I was proudly putting the finishing touches to my latest invention. Timed perfectly, as she began to remove her cardigan, I approached my teacher at her desk and presented my creation.

With the backdrop of chaos, as my noisy classmates piled into the room, taking their seats and exerting any remnants of excess energy they had left, I cleared my throat and announced over the rabble, "I finished it, Miss, here it is," tenderly placing my book in front of her.

Nonchalantly, she picked it up and examined the cover. I stood and waited for her reaction. A few seconds went by, and then a few more, a blank expression masked her face. She didn't say a word, she didn't even turn the first page. I was perplexed. I stood there, waiting for a sign of approval, something to assure me that my forfeited break had not been in vain.

Then she sat down and leant forward in her chair, putting the book back down, she began to scribble a note on the pad beside her. Similar to a doctor dispensing an urgent prescription, she stripped the page from the pad and ushered me out of the room, directing me to the classroom next door, book and note in hand.

As I stood confused in the doorway of 6P, Mr P spotted me looking out of place and waved me over. Reaching out for the note, I handed it to him as he leant back against his desk. He studied the note for some time before reaching out for my book in a non-audible gesture. I handed it over to him, attempting to establish eye contact but he looked past me.

I watched his eyes as he perused the cover, desperately searching his face for a hint of intrigue, delight, fascination… but nothing. Then quite unexpectedly, he let out an amused snigger, before handing the book back to me.

Confused, mixed with disappointment, I returned to class. I sat down at my desk, studying the cover of my book, searching for some explanation for the unusual chain of events that had just unfolded. As my teacher swept past me handing out textbooks for the commencement of the next lesson, she leant down and scoffed, "It should say written and illustrated by Nicola Morrison, not wrote!"

Startled by her sudden presence, I jumped. Pondering what she had just said, I looked back at the book cover and suddenly realised my error and the realisation of the meaning behind the bizarre ordeal I had just endured suddenly came into sharp focus. It had nothing to do with my book, my illustrations or my supposed ingenious plot twist as I had hoped. Instead, they had been mocking me for a typo and I had been the butt of their inside joke.

As my teacher stood at the front of the class and proceeded with the maths lesson, I felt a mixture of hurt, humiliation and anger bubbling up on the inside of me. Everything was a haze as I tried to bypass the pain in the pit of my stomach and tune into the audible frequency of the lesson, but everything sounded muffled. Overcome with emotion my surroundings began to fade into the background. Steadying myself, I took a deep breath and looked down at my book one last time.

Distracted, my blood pressure began to normalise as I adoringly flicked through the pages and gradually transcended back into the lives of my main characters. I watched as they popped up and came to life on every page. I read through the pages as the tension built with every scene and then to the end and the imaginative plot twist—Cecil, the Centipede had won the match against all odds! I smiled to myself, as I closed the last page. Placing my book in my desk drawer, I smiled to myself and reconciled that it was a good book, and it was their loss if they couldn't see that!

We moved to a new house again when I was seven and a half, to an area called Colindale. We lived on a new development on an estate in Burnt Oak. It was an area we had never heard of before and was at least a 30-minute drive away from anything that looked remotely familiar.

The flat was brand new, Sean and I had our own rooms, and we had a huge lounge-dining room and a detached garage. The block was built in an idyllic spot on the development, amongst other new-build properties with trees and greenery all around; it was beautiful. Not too far from the flat was a huge park that joined our estate with the 'bad' estate and in the middle was a huge log cabin and a climbing frame for all the kids on either side of the divide to convene.

The biggest highlight about moving to our new flat was the news that very soon we would be joined by a new addition to the family, and I would finally get to be a big sister.

For the entire duration of Mum's pregnancy, everyone had referred to the baby as 'he', and so I resigned myself to the fact that it was a done deal that I was having a little brother and had accepted it. So, you can imagine my amazement when Dad announced to us after school one day that Mum was in the hospital and had given birth to our new little sister. This was the best surprise ever!

That evening, Dad dressed us up in our Sunday best and attempted to cornrow (plait) my unruly, neglected hair to meet my new sibling. At the hospital, after I had washed my hands as instructed by Mum, I got to hold my little sister for the first time. Her eyes were closed tight shut and she made a light gurgling noise but didn't cry. She had a chubby face and wet-looking curls that covered the entirety of her head.

Sleeping peacefully, I looked down at her enamoured. It was official, I was in love.

The day Mum brought Camille home from the hospital was one of the best days of my life. I had a new companion, and as Mum set her down in her Moses basket in the lounge, I peered in, and at that moment, subconsciously I vowed to protect her with my life. I decided that if all the horrible life experiences I had faced up until this point meant that she could have a good life, it had all been worth it.

Having a new little sister was the best thing to happen to our family in a long time and in some ways brought me and Sean closer together for a short spell. We gravitated towards each other as we navigated our new surroundings and made friends with the neighbourhood kids. We met other siblings like us on the block and hung out in one big group, going on night bike rides and climbing trees, and onto roofs of garages and outbuildings.

That summer, I discovered computer games, and Sylvanian Families, and learnt how to ride a BMX bike, but most importantly, I learnt how to be a big sister.

I had always wanted a big sister, not to replace Sean, but just to have another girl around besides me. One that I could share secrets with and play with when I wanted to do girly things like braid my doll's hair or play dress up. I had always envied my friends with older sisters and admired that they had a built-in best friend, right under the same roof. I was assured by many sister-siblings that it wasn't all harmony and happy playdates, but undeterred, I wanted it all the same.

When Camille was born, I decided that not being able to have a big sister, but having a little sister was the next best thing and that I would instead become the big sister I had always wanted.

Mum affectionately called me the mother hen as I doted on my baby sister as attentively as if I had given birth to her myself. At age nine, I could change her nappy, use the right ratio of wipes vs zinc cream, heat and test her bottle, sterilise her dummies and pick her up out of her cot unaided. I also figured out how to make her stop crying by running the tap in the kitchen whilst holding her in my arms.

She would become fixated on the water shooting out of the faucet and almost instantly her tears would stop. When I told Mum that story years later, she humorously quipped and asked if that was why her water bill back then was so high!

Camille was a cute baby. Whenever we would take her out, it would take us twice as long to get the weekly shopping done as grannies would stop us in the street. I felt a sense of pride when they would gush and coo over her in her pram.

Things were almost perfect, and our family was almost complete, the only thing that was missing was Dad. Mum told us he had a girlfriend now and when she mentioned the name, I recognised it instantly. I had met her loads of times back at the big house.

We saw Dad less and less until almost a year had passed without contact. I missed him desperately and would cry myself to sleep most nights. I couldn't comprehend it. I used to be his baby girl and didn't understand how he could desert me.

One night, I was inconsolable and had cried myself ragged. My body involuntarily convulsing, Mum frantically tried to track him down, calling every phone number she had for him until she finally managed to locate him. And then less than an hour later, as if by magic, just as I was drifting off, he appeared by my bedside.

"Hey, Gum-Gum," he whispered in my ear. Semi-conscious and not quite sure if I was dreaming, I shot up in my bed.

"Dad!" I squealed as I threw my arms around him, vowing to never let go. He squeezed me back, kissing me and telling me over and over how much he loved me. He kept repeating that he was only ever a phone call away and that he would never leave me. Instantly, in that moment, I forgave him for everything. He hadn't abandoned me after all. It didn't matter that he and Mum didn't live under the same roof anymore, in fact, I preferred it.

We were happy for the peace and quiet. All that mattered was that he was here right now and that I was still his baby girl.

The next day when I came home from school, Mum told me that I had a special delivery and when I went into my bedroom, there were two medium-sized envelopes sitting on my bed. I tore them open in sheer excitement. They were cards, both from Dad. One was funny, with Garfield, the cat, on the front and had a humorous limerick complete with a punchline inside, that had me in fits of laughter and rolling about on my bed; typical dad!

The other one was more sentimental, illustrated with a solemn teddy bear on the front. Inside, he had written, declaring how important I was to him and how much he loved me. I stared at the teddy bear on the front as I wiped away my happy tears. He always knew just what to say and what to do to make me feel special; that was typical dad too.

At six months, my mum held a baby dedication for my sister at her parent's church. The ceremony was followed by a celebration at our home 'out in the sticks'. The flat was full to the brim with family and friends from both sides, everyone came, except Dad. My dad's brother brought his new girlfriend, Alison. She had beautiful pale, mixed-race skin, she reminded me of Mariah Carey, with cheeks that went pink when she blushed. She had a small perfect nose and lips and was smilcy and sweet but had a subtle confidence which I admired. I instantly warmed to her.

A few months later, when Mum put together my sister's Christening album, I smuggled Alison's photo out of it and took it to school. I told everyone that she was my long-lost big sister from America called Sharlyn. I wasn't sure at the time if anyone believed me, but deep down, I don't think I cared. I was indulging my fantasy, if only for a short time.

Over the years, Alison and I grew closer. She was intelligent, kind and warm, but could also hold her own amongst my more outspoken, unfiltered family members. She was a breath of fresh air and brought structure and fellowship to a dysfunctional dynamic, hosting random barbecues at their house and orchestrating games nights during the holidays. Her and Dad had a running tally of wins and defeats as they ignited one another's competitive streaks and would battle it out in their annual Christmas game of Scrabble.

It would go on for hours and had everyone gripped waiting to see who would be crowned champion and erupt into celebratory song, which we would have to endure until they returned to defend their title the following year. It was endearing to see Dad's playful side that instantly catapulted me back to the blissful memories of my childhood, watching him and Mum buoyantly sparring against one another.

Alison was always supportive and encouraging, especially when it came to my passion for writing.

If anyone took the time to ask me what I wanted to be when I grew up, without hesitation I would reply the same every time, "I'm going to be an author and illustrator of children's books." Most adults were so impressed with my focus and evident clarity on my future career plans that they would leave it there, but not Alison. Every time she would see me, she would enquire about my future prospects and show an interest in my latest creative writing feat or sketchbook.

Years later, when she got a job at a publishing house, she invited me to visit and told me that when I finished school, I could intern there. I loved that she was generous and genuinely cared. She had an adventurous, fun-loving energy that was almost as infectious as her trademark laugh.

4

Unorthodox

I often wonder if life would have been easier for me growing up if I had been more successful at fitting in, because for as long as I can remember, I just didn't—too outspoken, too opinionated, too strong-willed, too much of a tomboy, too energetic, too sensitive, too tough, too passionate! I just always seemed to be too much of something or not enough of something else. But I didn't know how to be anything other than myself, and as a very young child, for a long time, I didn't want to be either.

It was on a holiday with Mum, my siblings and some family friends at Sherwood Forest, when I discovered my love for BMX-biking. Trading in my initial choice of a Raleigh bike, I returned it for a dirt bike that resembled that of my brother and his peers. It was exhilarating exploring the dirt tracks and learning how to do wheelies. We practised stunts whilst jumping off sandbanks and free-falling down hills with my feet off the pedals.

I knew that my brother would only let me continue to hang out with him and his friends if I could keep up and showed no signs of weakness that could interfere with their daredevil antics. I did my best to not hold the male-dominated group back and be perceived as the weak link; despite my inner reservations, I followed suit, attempting risky stunts and cycling down steep, winding trails that levelled just inches away from a lagoon at the bottom. Suffering bruises and scrapes along the way, I hid the pain from my face for fear of being ousted.

In the years that followed, we began to spend more frequent weekends with Dad at his flat. It was then that I discovered where I got my thrill-seeking trait from and learnt that Dad had a passion for sports cars, evident from his living room which was littered with motoring car newspapers and glossy magazines. Sports cars framed the walls, and the TV was almost frozen on Formula 1 coverage for hours on end. It wasn't long before I too had adopted his passion for cars and was initiated into the world of petrol heads.

Every year, Dad would take Sean and me with him to Brands Hatch for the car show or to the drag racing tournaments at Santa Pod (think more Top Gear and less Rupaul!). I learnt about carburettors, catalytic converters, and car body kits. I felt completely at home, even though out of a group of Dad and Sean and Dad's friends and their sons, I was the only girl, but I didn't care. I liked being 'one of the lads'. It seemed easy to assimilate and I could just be me.

When Dad picked up a newer hobby of go-karting, Sean and I would accompany him and his friends and go along most weekends to watch him race. Often frequenting a greasy spoon café with Dad and his racing buddies after the tournament.

Go-karting was an un-glamourous, dirty life, and it was almost always cold and raining—all the things I hated, but somehow, I was able to overcome all of that for the chance to just relax and be myself, out of the spotlight of bullies and tormentors. Here I was simply accepted into the fold as all that was required was a mutual shared enthusiasm and I had loads of that!

I felt much more comfortable in these environments, where no one seemed to focus on my outward aesthetic. As a result, I gravitated more and more towards activities that provided high energy and escapism in equal measure, and after a brief encounter with my younger cousin's Super Nintendo console, my passion for computer games was also ignited.

The first computer game I had actually ever played was the Mummy game on Sean's Amstrad computer years before. This was back when computer consoles had keyboards and joysticks and the games came in the form of a cassette tape and took an entire 30 minutes to load. I fondly reminisce about all the times Sean, and I would speed through dinner, eating at lightning speed, excited at the prospect that our long-awaited game would finally be fully loaded and ready to be played.

The first console I owned was a Sega Mega Drive. Nan and Grandad M bought it for my eighth or ninth birthday as a surprise—I was overjoyed. Holed up in my room for hours, I would try to perfect my skills as I manoeuvred the spikey blue hedgehog on the screen to jump, run and fly through the air in a bid to collect as many gold rings as possible.

I became obsessed with completing each level of the game with not only the highest score on the leaderboard but also with the most lives intact. My perfectionism often drove me to play the game all day and all night, or at least until Mum told me I had reached my playing limit for the day, and it was time to unplug.

In defiance, on the weekends I would wake up at ungodly hours of the morning to complete my challenge and like a well-rehearsed ritual, gently switch on my TV and simultaneously hit the mute button on the remote control to ensure that my early ascent remained undetected. I would then play until my heart's content, glued to the screen, controller in hand, poised on the edge of my bed, still in my pyjamas, long into the afternoon.

Dad had a less sophisticated PC computer at his flat, with basic platform games, which Sean and I would un-amicably take turns playing, Solitaire, Minesweeper or the more challenging quests of the Prince of Persia.

One weekend, Dad presented me with a belated birthday present of a karaoke machine, and to Sean's relief, I was distracted from the computer for an entire weekend whilst I graced the entire household and neighbourhood with my dulcet tones as my karaoke speaker box blasted out to the soundtrack of *Careless Whisper* on repeat.

Dad always had a new hobby, and no matter what it was, he had to have the latest gear. On one weekend visit, he told us that he had started taking video production classes and showed us his new state-of-the-art camera kit that he had recently purchased. From then on, most weekends with Dad were spent assisting him hone his production skills, whilst he made home videos—following us around the house or on short trips to the park, often directing us for comedic effect.

We enjoyed being the stars of the show, although we did not always understand the farcical value of what we were doing or saying, nonetheless, we were happy to go along with it.

Years later, we discovered the archive of these home videos and spent hours watching them back and were thoroughly entertained by our out-of-date fashions and now comprehendible Dad-scripted anecdotes.

Undeniably, summer held the best memories of my childhood. My siblings and I spent most of our summers bouncing around the homes of family members or at summer playscheme whilst Mum worked.

My favourite place of all during the season was with my mum's eldest brother and his family, which included my favourite cousin Chris, who was six years older than me, his mum and his two older brothers.

At Chris' house, we spent our long summer days at the park or hanging out in the back garden. They had a large patio deck with sun loungers and the rest of the garden was landscaped with an apple tree and a frog pond.

We would play 'keepy uppies' with a football—a game where you have to try to keep the ball in the air by bouncing it against various parts of the body: foot, knee, shoulder, head, before skilfully passing it on to someone else in the circle. I was only ever able to keep it up with a maximum of two consecutive bounces, but they humoured me all the same by allowing me to join in, if only for a brief contribution.

Indoors we would play computer games to the soundtrack of RnB music that would blare out of their back-bedroom window. I soon learnt that hanging with my brother and much older male cousins came at a price and that being both the youngest and the only girl meant that I was often in the firing line for a random roasting. With time, I was soon able to master the skill of banter and provide quick-witted retorts in my defence, which often left them all stunned and falling about laughing in amazement.

It was official, I had earned my right of passage. I was in!

Hanging out with my brother and big cousins, we whiled away the time playing vinyl records and they taught me all about all different genres of music; Hip Hop, RnB, Soul and Acoustic and schooled me on the artistry of KRS-One, Naughty by Nature and The Wu-Tang Clan.

Sometimes, if I promised to be extra careful, they would allow me the privilege of 'dropping the needle' to start the record track. However, I was soon stripped of my record-starting rights when my not-so-nimble fingers lost their grip on the needle, suddenly causing one of their coveted records to be scratched. It would be weeks before they would trust me with the assignment again.

In the meantime, I attempted to practice my craft whenever I was left unsupervised and discovered that if I turned the fader down during transitions, I could conceal any potential indiscretions, by only turning the volume up once the song was in full swing.

For some of the summer, we would go to a summer playscheme. Sean and I would split ranks. He would gravitate towards outdoor activities; playing football, racing with newfound friends or mounting the complex and most challenging climbing frame structures in the playground. Whilst I would retreat to one of the classrooms to participate in a painting activity, decorating a mural or making a pin cushion out of squares of felt.

When Mum would come to collect us, we were never in the same place. Sean would be ripping around the playground with his friends, and I would be tucked away in deep concentration in the arts and crafts room.

Throughout the six weeks of playscheme, they would plan regular excursions—the Natural History Museum, a steam engine train ride in the countryside, and a picnic at Box Hill. With every letter of consent asking for payment and a signature that we brought home, Mum would try to curtail our expensive appetite for adventure and remind us that she could not fulfil all our requests if we were to go on the end of summer annual camping trip.

The camping trip to The New Forest was the summer finale and without fail, within 24 hours of admissions opening, happy campers rushed back to playscheme with their signed letters and payments in hand for a space on the highly sought-after trip.

Registration was over, our names were down, and it was official we were going. Sean was ecstatic and I was secretly dreading it. Camping was a world away from anything we had ever experienced—abseiling, kayaking, hiking and for everything that Sean loved about our new experience, I loathed. Sean adapted quickly to the outdoorsy life and made friends. I found it harder to bond with my peers, who seemed completely unperturbed by the intermittent weather and showed no discomfort in being cold, dirty or wet – all of my pet peeves.

The food was unsavoury and unappetising, and whilst Sean and his friends survived the week on a pooled collection of biscuits, chocolates and sweets, my tent buddies were less of a collective, so I grazed the table in the main marquee and most nights went to bed hungry.

The cold mornings were the worst, my slim frame providing minimal insulation. I resigned myself to wearing all of the outerwear clothes in my duffle bag before heading to the freezing cold communal showers. My greatest highlight of each day was the 30 minutes before bed, when we sat with the camp leaders around a roaring campfire, drinking hot cocoa, and toasting marshmallows. It was safe to say camping was my least favourite thing about summer.

5

In the Mirror

Who is that girl in the mirror, looking back at me, devoid of happiness, lacking love and beauty, alone and ashamed; what is the name of the girl looking back at me?

Growing up, no one ever told me I was pretty. I would see other children being complimented on their appearance as they turned out in their Sunday best for church. "Aren't you handsome young man!" The elders of the church would say.

"Well, isn't that a beautiful dress young lady!" They would gush. But I never seemed to capture their admiration.

Beauty according to Mum was not to be held in high regard or any regard for that matter. We were commended for being smart, polite and well-mannered, or for doing our chores and helping out. We were taught that the things that mattered were that you were a good person, that you were intelligent and well accomplished, and that being pretty just in and of itself was not a valuable commodity in life.

Instead, it was instilled in us that our worth was defined by our minds and our hearts, not what was on the outside, which for a long time was a sentiment that went unchallenged, until I got older and was exposed to the opinions of others on my outward appearance.

Unexpectedly and quite unprepared, I was suddenly thrust into an arena where I was constantly confronted by others about my aesthetic imperfections. I couldn't escape the constant ridicule of my dad's relatives, who would mock me and liken my build to Olive Oil in Popeye or refer to me with derogatory names like 'mawga' and 'kadunkum'—Jamaican patois terms which allude to the skinny, unattractive frame of a woman, which according to them, I qualified for.

The boys at school would mock me and liken the colour of my skin to faeces and my hair to Medusa. For the first time, I was made aware that I had big lips, and that in the eyes of my taunters, this was also bad.

It seemed every part of my existence seemed to warrant some form of ridicule. Looking in the mirror, I was suddenly confronted with a completely different image from what I had seen before. Fixating on my features that had now become my flaws, I obsessed.

Before now, I had never considered my outward appearance or contemplated the value of my outward beauty. So focused on being the best person I could be on the inside, I had neglected to pay attention to the exterior, and now to my surprise, I discovered I had fallen short. Without warning or inclination, the jury had ruled, and the verdict was in, and it was official, I didn't meet the mark; I was ugly!

Then one day out of the blue, my hair started falling out. This wasn't just light shedding or broken ends, it started to fall out in clumps from the root, leaving patches all over my head. My scalp became inflamed and sensitive to the touch, and all the lotions and potions my mum experimented with only seemed to make things worse. Week after week, I would be taken to visit a different specialist or holistic scalp guru, but not one of them seemed to be able to diagnose my condition or more importantly provide a cure.

My scalp was sore to the touch as boils began to form across my entire head and erupt all over it, like little angry inflamed volcanoes. The patches of missing hair became impossible to disguise. As if I wasn't already enough of a target, my tormentors now had another weapon in their arsenal and as a result, I was subjected to sniggers and jibes as I sat in assembly or on my walk home.

It was around this time that I began harbouring what a therapist would undoubtedly diagnose as an unhealthy obsession with the natural beauty and talent of Mariah Carey. I had figured it all out and managed to convince myself that waking up and being transformed into her would solve all my problems. The boys at school would no longer see me as ugly or Black, which in my mind, from the constant bullying and teasing, had become one and the same.

I would no longer have my horrible, wispy, frizzy, mousy-brown hair, but instead, it would be replaced with beautiful, flowing, golden-blonde ringlets. I would be the perfect height and build, no longer too tall or too skinny. I would have the perfect sized lips and complexioned skin; it was the perfect solution. "Lord, just make me Mariah Carey!" I prayed—it would all be so simple.

On one of my many hangouts with Chris, I quizzed him in my typical philosophical-reporter-like fashion (I was truly always destined to be a journalist) and asked him, "If you could be anyone in the world who would you be?"

And to my surprise, without even missing a beat, he profoundly replied, "If you're not happy being you, you will never be happy in life!"

I was floored. I couldn't even imagine being so content in life that I would pass up the opportunity to be someone else, even if it was just hypothetical! In an ideal world that would have been the reality check I needed to set me back on course, and never contemplate wanting to be someone else ever again. But it was already too late.

The constant physical assaults and verbal ridicule I had endured at school, coupled with relentless critiquing from certain family members had already begun to manifest in me a deep self-loathing. I was no longer the confident, happy-go-lucky, upbeat personality I had always been. They had beaten me down, and what hadn't been destroyed physically had been emotionally. I needed a new reflection in the mirror, because the one I currently had, had been rejected by the world.

6

Growing Pains

Over the next few years, the time we spent with Dad became more and more sporadic. He would show up unannounced at the school gates or intercept us as we got off the bus and walked home. In the beginning, we relished the opportunity to spend time with him. But with every encounter, I was left more disappointed by the lack of quality time to be had.

Our evenings with him often consisted of being strapped in the car for hours as he made endless pit stops or sent us on mundane errands, picking up something for him from the local auto garage or making a purchase at a sports shop.

On these misadventures after school, we would often end up at the local sports centre. He had lost interest in his former passion for bodybuilding and was now an avid squash player, competing in tournaments, friendly matches and even coaching a junior squad. He no longer ran the video business either, and we weren't always exactly sure where he was living or with whom.

My siblings and I would amuse ourselves, running around the establishment's maze-like layout, and playing hide and seek. I always felt self-conscious of how much we stood out amongst the fitness fanatics in their sports attire as we frolicked about into the hours of the night, still in our school uniforms—our unscheduled visit evident to all.

The rest of the time was spent being Daddy's little helpers, ferrying his kit and equipment back and forth. Before heading home, if the odds were in our favour and we timed it just right when we asked, he would give us a couple of pounds each to get a portion of chips and a slush puppy from the canteen. Other times, we would return home hungry.

At the end of the evening, he would drop us off at the garden gate, the hour now well past our bedtime and speed off, as we would be greeted by a frazzled

Mum at the front door. Feelings of despondency mounted inside of me, as I undressed for bed and unpacked a pile of neglected homework from my rucksack, hungry and disappointed.

We never really knew when we would see Dad again, so when he would call out of the blue on the weekend and announce that he was on his way to get us, we dropped everything to make ourselves available. Our enthusiasm came very much to Mum's frustration, causing her to abandon her Saturday plans and reschedule appointments. Unable to reason with us with warnings of potentially missing friends' birthday parties or having to cancel scheduled playdates, she would reluctantly give in to our pleas, accepting defeat.

Being able to see Dad, in our eyes, trumped everything. The house would erupt into chaos as we hung up the phone, following his surprise announcement. The countdown began as his pending arrival drew closer and closer and we raced around the house to ensure we would be ready on time. We knew only too well that he would not wait.

Following the record-breaking dash, everything became still as we sat on the staircase in anticipation. Bathed, pruned and groomed, we waited patiently for Dad to arrive. As the minutes turned into hours, the excitement and anticipation ebbed away, slowly replaced by hopelessness and devastation, as the realisation that he was not coming began to sink in. After some time had passed, Mum would try to call him on the phone, over and over, but to no avail.

Fighting back tears of frustration, she would dismiss us from our sacred waiting place and would try to console us with promises of being able to salvage what was left of our weekend. Stomping and sobbing on the way up to my room, I would vocalise my frustration, vowing never to forgive him for letting me down again. And this time, I swore I meant it, at least until the next time.

Each time we would do the same 'dance'. The innocence of youth ensured that each time he called and announced he was en route, unperturbed by the disappointments and letdowns of the past, we repeated the same charade. When on occasion he would show up, sometimes he would take us with him, other times he would dismiss us at the gate and drive away claiming he didn't like how Mum had dressed us or how she had styled our hair.

Now embroiled in a bitter divorce, we were left exposed in the crossfire of our parents' warfare and the irreparable destruction of our family. Sometimes I questioned whether they even noticed me or if I was just collateral damage amidst tactical game-playing. Defenceless, we were thrust onto an emotional rollercoaster, with no means of getting off. We had no choice but to continue to ride it out, and so each time he called, we prayed and waited.

As I got older, I began to feel more conflicted about going with Dad when he showed up out of the blue. I would hesitate to get in the car, with protests of after-school activities and homework deadlines when he intercepted me en route home. Sometimes I felt like he liked putting us in the middle, attempting to persuade me with promises of fun expeditions followed by a hearty meal. And when I flat-out refused, he threatened that he would disown me and never speak to me again. Regardless of his method, he always got his way.

I never shared with friends at school how bad things between my parents had gotten since their separation. Everyone else's home lives seemed so perfect, I was embarrassed and ashamed to tell them about the chaotic, dysfunctionality of mine.

So, it was like divine intervention when unexpectedly one of my school friends lent me a book, she had gotten from a book club. The book was by Judy Blume and was called *It's Not the End of the World*—a story about a family going through separation and the tumultuous happenings of divorce from the perspective of the main character, the middle child of the family, Karen. The story followed her as she battled through the stages of denial, grief, and then finally, acceptance.

I felt like I could completely relate to Karen, more than any living being, at that time. It was as if the words on the pages of the book were playing out my life story. I read that book over and over at least twenty times and every time I did it was as though I was having an intimate conversation with the author, who somehow knew me intrinsically.

She was speaking directly to me and into my situation—the characters expressing emotions I shared but lacked the words to articulate, proved comforting as I read the book alone in bed each night. I held on to the promise from Ms Blume that this wouldn't be the end of the world, even if right now it felt like it!

Our visits with Dad continued to be infrequent and unscheduled throughout the years, but if there was one thing we could be sure of, it was that we would always be guaranteed a visit for birthdays. He would show up to a hero's welcome at the front door as he offloaded elaborate giftings from his car boot— a coloured TV, roller skates, the designer puffer jacket I had always wanted.

Standing in the doorway, I was filled with a burst of elation, and then he was gone again, until the next time.

Despite this, somehow, we never questioned him and his erratic parenting style or dared to hold it against him, afraid to rock the boat and as a consequence the intervals between visits be extended even longer. Instead, we learnt to live in the moment and just bask in his company, no matter how brief. Gifts were his love language and we accepted that and cherished his presents as an extension of his presence.

My favourite childhood present of all time was from my dad. He surprised me with a Mickey Mouse and Goofy character set, complete with a storybook, as a Christmas gift. They were an impressive two feet tall each and had tape cassettes that plugged into their backs and leads that plugged into a speaker. They talked and blinked as they interacted and told the story of a fictional explorer called Stan Livingstone. It was like nothing I had ever seen before.

I was mesmerised as I would sit and watch their eyes open and close, and their motorised mouths move up and down in sync with the audio. I received many special gifts over the years, but they were undoubtedly on the list of my most cherished. I didn't part with them until I was well into my teens, long after I had misplaced the tape cassette and Mickey's eyelids no longer blinked in unison!

As much as I loved my gifts from my dad, as cliché as it sounds, nothing in my mind beat spending time with him and I would've traded it all in an instant for that. But I was conflicted. I knew in my heart of hearts I didn't want Mum and Dad to get back together again. I went as far as to tell them so, threatening that I and my teddy bears would pack up and leave if they even contemplated reconciling. But I wished for some way that they could coexist, at least for long enough so that we could spend time together and do things that other normal families did.

I knew this was an impossible dream and any fantasies of harmonious bliss amongst my parents were pushed even further from my reality when Dad showed up one evening unannounced and beckoned for us to come outside. And there, on the pavement, under the streetlights and out of Mum's earshot, he told us that our little half-brother had been born.

In the summer of 1995, we moved again when Mum bought a house in the heart of sub-urban Wembley. For the first time in a long time, the move felt permanent. Our Wembley postcode was in a family-orientated community in a safe and friendly neighbourhood, and we were surrounded in a one-street radius by family and friends.

The new home was a charming, yet modest, 1940s terrace house on a quiet street at the end of a network of roads that intersected into one another. Inside the décor was a little dated, but it had potential. The upstairs bedrooms were all a decent size, and there were two large reception rooms on the ground-floor and a galley kitchen that led out onto an impressive, yet manageable-sized garden. It felt like home.

In no time at all, Mum had completely gutted the place, remodelling one room at a time. She was committed to putting her personal stamp on her new purchase and executing her vision with exact precision. For months, we spent every weekend trawling through Home Depot and DIY shops whilst she chose curtain fabrics, carpets, wallpaper and fixtures and fittings. The house was constantly overrun with builders, plumbers and plasterers, and when she ran out of money and couldn't afford to pay for any more labourers, she hired the tools and did it herself.

We spent an entire weekend completing the back-breaking, arduous task of removing the hallway wallpaper with a manual steamer she had rented. Balancing precariously over the staircase banister, we became increasingly astounded as we stripped off layer after layer until we finally finished in the late evening, convinced that a century's worth of wallpaper lay in shreds at our feet.

I could see it was hard for Mum, doing it all on her own, and some days the pressure and financial strain of homemaking for a family of four by herself took its toll. But then with every completed room and finishing touch, a happiness was ignited inside of her, that somehow re-energised her and motivated her to keep going.

As her vision came to fruition, she reminded us that all the sacrifices had been worth it; all the jobs she'd had to take whilst leaving us to go to work, all the scrimping and saving and living on a budget, all of it had led up to this moment, and now we were finally here in a 'proper' home.

When guests would come to visit, she would leap into action. Full of excitement, she would take them on a grand tour, stopping to point out the intricate details of the mahogany cabinets in the bathroom or to impart a historical fact about the uniqueness of the grain of the kitchen countertops. Hours after they had left, I would catch her in her own little world, still walking from room to room, admiring her interior design touches, beaming with pride as she examined the impressive workmanship of her handpicked finishes, marvelling at her epic feat, now complete.

She was especially touched when Grandad M came to visit and commended her on her achievement, giving her his enthused seal of approval.

Grandad M understood better than most what it took to see a vision through, and the grit and determination it took to persevere. From humble beginnings in Kingston Jamaica, he had arrived in the UK and managed against all odds to establish himself as a business owner. He was the first person I knew that owned his own shop; a dry-cleaning business in a Black-Caribbean community in the heart of Harlesden, North West London. It was an accomplishment for all of us, he was setting down roots and building a legacy.

When we were still attending junior school, our childminder would drop us off at his dry cleaners at the end of the day, and later after work, Mum would come and pick us up. As I would enter the establishment and walk across the shop floor, I would take great pride in walking past unsuspecting customers, before lifting the hatch and proceeding to walk behind the counter.

Like a VIP at an exclusive hangout, I could go where others were forbidden. I felt proud of Grandad M and privileged to be his granddaughter. He was undoubtedly my favourite person. A tall man with a friendly giant persona. His build was broad, his presence was domineering, coupled with a deep, gruff voice. In the early years, I was terrified of him on account of his big stature and booming voice and would shy away from him whenever he entered the room or tried to engage with me.

But over the years, I couldn't help but gravitate towards him, as I would observe him at the shop after school, during quiet times, delicately mending garments on a sewing machine in the backroom, glasses perched on the end of his nose in deep concentration under the bright light of his table lamp. I saw the gentler side of him as he laughed and joked with friends that visited and began to appreciate his sense of humour and distinguish what he was saying, through his thick Jamaican accent.

He would take me for rides around the area in his sports car and give me money to buy food from the local chicken shop or a patty and dumpling from the Caribbean haunt up the hill. He was enthused when he discovered I didn't know what a chip butty was and delighted in taking me to the local chippie before bringing me back to the shop and preparing with great enthusiasm and precision his 'must-try' snack.

It was in the company of Grandad M that my love for comedy was birthed. Soon after arriving at his home, I would abandon guests in the through lounge, being entertained by Nan to climb the stairs and join him upstairs watching telly in the confines of the master bedroom. Sprawled out on the bed in his silk pyjama bottoms and string vest, and remote in hand, as I entered the room, I would be greeted by his roaring laughter as he entertained himself watching comedy shows on his video recorder. I would clamber up onto the bed beside him as he watched his favourite stand-up comics and sketch shows for hours on end.

Grandad M loved his downtime, but when he was on, he was the life and soul of the party; he was animated, fun-loving and would hold the attention of the entire room. He would often invite me into his sacred man cave in the attic, where he spent time with his old-timer friends and they would play reggae music and ska all night, whilst he showcased his extensive record collection. Reggae and Lover's Rock became the soundtrack of my childhood, The Wailers, Tippa Irie, and Janet Kay's music even to this day brings back a warm and cosy feeling of nostalgia.

Music was a welcome distraction from the realities of life and spending time with Grandad M just made it even better. He made me feel protected. He was one of the only adults at the time that I can truly say saw me and loved me unconditionally, and I loved him right back.

Then one day after rehearsals for the Christmas play, we were unusually dropped off by our childminder to Granny and Grandad S's house instead of to the shop. When we went inside, they told us to sit down and proceeded to tell us that Grandad M had collapsed and was in the hospital. We all sat in silence in the living room as Granny and Grandad S fielded phone calls and received updates on the telephone in the hallway.

Later that evening, Mum collected us and took us to the hospital, and we met Dad and the rest of the family there. I scanned Dad's face and it immediately registered that I had never seen him carry such a sombre expression. As I entered the family room, I was struck by the palpable feeling of grief in the air and tears almost instantly began streaming from my eyes. I didn't know the prognosis or even what a brain haemorrhage was, but the knot in my stomach confirmed to me in an instant that this was bad.

Mum and Dad led Sean and me over to an almost deserted ward and over to Grandad M's hospital bed. I was speechless as I looked on to see my bestie, once larger than life and full of energy, now almost unrecognisable, still and lifeless in a coma. Glued to the spot, I stared at him whilst he lay there motionless, tears blurring my vision whilst I wrestled with God in my head, pleading with him to wake me up from this nightmare.

As we left later that night and I walked across the hospital car park and got into the car, I remember feeling immediately enraged as Mum switched on the engine and we were confronted with festive Christmas tunes blaring out of the radio. I couldn't believe how inappropriate it now felt to even consider that anyone anywhere could possibly be thinking about celebrating Christmas against the backdrop of our new reality.

We visited Grandad M in the hospital every day after school. As he lay unconscious in his hospital bed, I looked around his room, decorated with birthday cards filled with well-wishes and prayers, and then like a sharp jolt to the abdomen, it hit me—he was never going to get to read them, he was never going to know how much we were willing him to wake up, because he wasn't going to wake up. I felt the shattering of my heart as it broke into a million pieces. Two weeks later, he died.

Some of Grandad M's brothers flew in from the US and Jamaica, and one of his brothers whom I had never met before resembled him remarkably. It was uncanny, having had no knowledge of him just weeks before, I found myself almost immediately gravitating towards him, sitting on his lap at the house and beside him at the infamous nine-night (Jamaican wake), desperate to absorb every familial intonation of his voice and reminiscent facial expression.

Grandad M's friends were in shock and utter disbelief, and it was almost chilling to see a group of men that I had only ever known to be jovial and upbeat now with permanently solemn faces, overcome with grief. I cried throughout the entire funeral service and at one point, had to be taken out by a family friend so that I could compose myself.

After Grandad M died, his house never felt the same again. Now confined to the living room when we visited, I no longer ventured up the staircase, which once led to a thrilling getaway.

We never visited the shop again after he died and somehow, I just knew everything would be different, forever.

Eight months later, our family suffered another untimely blow when Grandad S suffered a massive heart attack and passed away. It was more than I could bear. Both of my parents were grief-stricken. Consumed by the overwhelming weight of my sorrow, all I could do was stand by and watch as both sides of my family began to collapse under the weight of their anguish. Like a house being eroded by the relentless, crashing waves of the sea, the very foundation of my family began to subside and disintegrate, until there was almost nothing left.

For some people, grandparents are just distant relatives that they only see a couple of times a year and that send hideous festive jumpers in the post at Christmas time. But my grandparents were so much more than that to me. They were like extended parents, and in an instant, two of them had been ripped away from me. It was too much for my 11-year-old brain to process.

Soon after, I began experiencing debilitating anxiety. My frequent and unprovoked panic attacks would strike with no prior warning at random intervals during the day or grip me in the middle of the night, thrusting me out of my sleep in a panic-stricken frenzy, heart racing, gasping for air. I didn't tell anyone about my episodes and suffered in secret as they went on to plague my existence for the next twenty-five years.

7

Broke

Having completely run out of money*; emotionally* overwhelmed.

The autumn after my grandads died, I started high school. I didn't tell any of my newfound friends about my recent months of hell. But instead, when I was asked by my form tutor to stand up and introduce myself to my new classmates, I spoke about my passion for acting and street dance, and my desire to become an author one day.

I saw high school as a chance to put everything behind me—my anxiety, my grief, memories of my bullies as well as my deep-seated feelings of abandonment by my dad, and my angst surrounding my fractured relationship with my mum. I was determined that high school would be a fresh start for me.

My new high school was intimidatingly grand. The grounds resembled a mixture between a stately home and a high-end boarding school. The buildings were architecturally impressive. All the classrooms were situated in one of four multi-storey, high-rise red brick buildings, called 'schoolhouses'. Each house was personalised with a corresponding colour and personalised name, which was carved into a plaque, suspended above each building's main entrance.

I was assigned to Herkomer House, the red house, which was the first of the four houses on the grounds and was joined to the other three by a 200-foot-long cloister. The brickwork along the cloister formed a mirror effect of a column of arches all the way down it, interrupted midway by a slabbed path that led to the main dining room and further along the path a grand assembly hall.

Plaques, medals and photos adorned the walls of the grand hall. Mahogany-stained wood panelling ran vertically along the wall of the interior. A one-metre-high stage, only accessible by steps to the right, commanded the attention of the room, drawing all eyes towards it on entry; the marvelling of the spectacle only ever slightly impeded by the piercing bright sunshine that shone down from the skylight, causing the solid, pine wood flooring to glisten and sparkle, and onlookers to blink and squint as the room became illuminated.

The grandeur of my new school was worlds apart from anything I had ever experienced before and I was well aware that I was a long way from home, both figuratively and literally!

The journey to my new school was no small undertaking and consisted of a 20-minute walk to the bus stop, followed by a 15-minute bus ride to the tube station, followed by a 30-minute train ride, and then another 20 minutes on another bus. By any commuting standards, but especially for that of an 11-year-old, it was a mission, to say the least. Especially when I compared it to the six-minute walk most of my friends in the neighbourhood took to get to the local high school.

Although my hopes of attending there were never a fully formed idea as Mum had long since made it clear she wanted her children to go to a 'good school', which in her opinion meant an institution with a remarkable reputation, an advanced academic offering as well as an impressive ranking on the league table. Unfortunately, the school up the road on the hill fell short on all accounts, and as a result, Sean and I were shipped off out of the area.

At my new high school, I encountered a predominantly White population, teachers and pupils alike. A less diverse demographic than my previous junior school, however, I somehow felt less disenfranchised and othered by my new environment. Some of my new classmates lived in what was deemed to be the undesirable part of town and knew some form of hardship, others came from one-parent homes or with parents who were working class and lived on a more conservative budget, which was a welcome contrast to my previous schooling experience.

Money at home was still tight, although Mum had managed to get a promotion at work to pay the mortgage, we were barely making ends meet, so she attempted to offset mounting household bills and the financial demands of being a single mother of three with an additional weekend part-time job. It wasn't as bad financially as it had been previously at the big house, but we were by no means out of the red, and designer clothes, expensive dinners and luxury holidays were things we only encountered in our dreams.

I saved up my pocket money to buy the things I wanted but didn't need. Mum took care of the essentials: school shoes, homework supplies, stationery and ingredients for cookery class. I purchased the fun stuff—CDs, lip gloss, arts and crafts, and pop magazines. Mum gave me some freedom to purchase my own clothes and fortunately for her, she was able to avoid the usual parent versus pre-teen changing room saga, which I had witnessed erupting into raised voices behind pulled curtains, followed by the emergence of a red-faced, exasperated parent shouting in the direction of the dressing room, "Well, you're not wearing that!"

The concept of short miniskirts and tight-fitting or revealing clothing did not appeal to me and instead, I often gravitated towards baggy joggers and oversized sweatshirts, to disguise my slim frame. My limited budget caused me to have to settle for four stripes instead of the authentic, higher-priced branded clothing with just three, but I resolved it was better than nothing and just hoped and prayed that no one would notice.

My older cousins would sometimes lend me their designer garments for special occasions, on the condition that the item was returned in pristine condition. And so, I guarded their cherished apparel as if my life depended on it, all the while knowing that future potential loans of items from their wardrobes were contingent on my safeguarding capabilities.

On Sundays after church, I journeyed on foot down the road to the infamous Wembley market. Once there, I immersed myself for hours amongst the sea of aisles, scouring the fashion racks for an elusive bargain. Time would fly by whilst I meandered back and forth between stalls, memorising sale points and negotiated discounts as I bartered with savvy market traders. Reluctant to part with my coveted savings, I would take my leave to give ample consideration prior to making my purchase, vowing to return if I couldn't find it cheaper elsewhere.

Spending money was the area that made me most hesitant. When it came to decision-making, I often felt confident and self-assured in my resolve, and at times even impulsive, except for when it came to parting with my moolah! It always gave me pause for thought and it didn't matter whether I was spending £1 at the sweetshop or £100 of my birthday money on a stunning typewriter or art set, I always had to give the process deep consideration. I had learnt how hard money was to come by and knew only too well the all too familiar feeling of not having any, so the idea of giving it away was one I did not entertain lightly.

As I browsed the sellers' spoils of Wembley market, the gravity of the situation bore down on me, and I began to make a mental tally of the pros and cons surrounding my potential purchase.

Did I really need it? Could I do without it? Would it make me happy? Or would I have buyer's remorse? And if I did buy it, what would be the state of my depleted funds?

The answers to my list of questions would determine whether or not I would proceed with the purchase, based on if my potential buy had satisfied the checklist I had created in my head.

It was not uncommon that by the time I had finished dithering and pondering and had finally come to the decision to part with my funds, the shopping period had ceased, and the market officials had taken to the megaphone to announce that the market was now closed and were asking all shoppers to make their way to the nearest exit.

Like a vigilante on the run, I ran, weaving in and out of the aisles, walking against the direction of the footfall, shapeshifting to avoid loading vans and cars as they entered the site to begin deconstruction as I attempted to locate the stall I was looking for.

The clanging of metal poles could be heard in chorus across the market as traders dismantled their stalls followed by the crinkling sound of tarp being rolled and folded. Sprinting through the marketplace, I tried to recall the precise location of my desired destination from earlier, my navigation skills now impeded by the disrupted gridlines of now vacant plots and idling vehicles. Panting and running, by some miracle, I arrived at my sought-after stall just as the market trader was zipping up his bum bag, stuffed full of paper notes and jingling pound coins.

As he turned to face me, he smiled, and his gold tooth came into view and glistened in the afternoon sun. "Ah just in time, young lady!" He exclaimed.

"Yes," I spluttered, out of breath, squeezing my left side which was now exhibiting a full-blown stitch.

He walked towards the back of the stall and approached a red and white candy-striped carrier bag, perched on a bar stool. "I thought you'd be back," he said. As he walked towards it.

Reaching for the bag, he said over his shoulder, "What did we say, £30?" He enquired.

£30? I thought. I had been wearing out these battered old trainers trying to find their replacement for the last two hours. We had haggled and bartered, and

I had managed to get him to knock down the price to £25 and now it seemed in the final hour, sensing my desperation he was trying to renegotiate.

Deflated but with hardly any breath in my lungs to argue, I felt the acceptance of defeat wash over me as I stood looking at his now fully turned back. With what little energy I had left, I replied sheepishly, "You said £25, we definitely agreed on £25."

As he turned to face me and passed me the bag, he knowingly winked and said with a cheeky grin, "Go on then!" reaching out his hand.

I beamed back and let out a sigh of relief. I handed over a sweaty and crumpled up £20 and £5 note. "Thank you!" I shouted as I ran off into the distance before he could change his mind!

The wide-ranging variance in the socio-economic groups amongst my new classmates at my new school helped to level the playing field and diminished any financial pressure I had felt previously.

What was also refreshing was that my academic year had the largest intake of Black children in the history of the school. It appeared many parents had the same idea as mine and several of the students that looked like me at intake, came from postcodes close to my neighbourhood.

Despite a less tense and racially divided school environment, there always seemed to be a simmering tension that bubbled just below the surface. The Asian kids kept to themselves, the Black kids and the White kids were often segregated in their social groups at break times, and there always seemed to be a sense of our presence as the Black kids being tolerated rather than wholly accepted, teaching staff included. There were a few exceptions.

Mrs Robinson, my English teacher, was my favourite. She was quiet and shy but made learning so engaging, her passion for literacy was so evident that I couldn't help but feel enthused and inspired by her. I thoroughly enjoyed it when she set us creative writing assignments and taught us about metaphors and similes.

Mr Henley, my drama teacher, came in a close second. His lessons were always so imaginative and exciting. I loved his playfulness and watching the creative cogs of his brilliant mind at work. I watched in awe as he would set the scene and fill an empty space with the words of his imagination or transport us to a different place and time just with the use of his descriptive prowess.

But other teachers were not so inviting and seemed to have not taken kindly to the influx of children of colour that had unexpectedly descended on their school from North West London.

My science teacher, an ex-army sergeant, would intentionally hold the Black students back at the end of the day for detention for the most minor infraction, whilst dismissing our White counterparts for similar contraventions. When we would protest that due to his unfair delays, we would now have to make our lengthy journeys home in the dark, he would make flippant comments, implying we should've attended a local school instead.

The sports staff talked down to the Black students and only seemed to regard them with any value when we were exhibiting athletic ability. An otherwise hostile Netball coach only acknowledged my existence when I scored a goal or won a sporting competition, and when I quit the team, the entire sports department gave me the silent treatment and I was banned from attending any social events held in the gymnasium.

The racial offences I experienced there seemed to be birthed from a place of ignorance rather than the more sinister, targeted encounters I had experienced at primary school, although aggressions, nonetheless. I was regularly bombarded with requests from my White peers to touch my hair and fielded questions, asking why it didn't 'fall down'? and how often did I wash it? Which only served as a reminder that I was different and didn't belong.

The feeling of not fitting in was further compounded by the stark reality that I also didn't seem to belong amongst those that looked like me either—a small minority of a dozen or more Black students, mostly female that spanned three academic years, mine, the one above me and the one above that. They had formed somewhat of a commuting community, and we all travelled the lengthy journey to school together. Small in size, this was, however, an undeniably divisive group, powerful in establishing or retracting your social status at a whim, a tight-knit circle that I frequently found myself on the outside of.

On a day much like any other, I met the group at break time beside the tuck shop as they congregated on the lawn devouring their recent sweet treat purchases. As I approached and gave a collective 'Hi' almost immediately I detected something wasn't right. No one responded to my greeting, an awkward silence hovered in the air and the tension became palpable. I looked around the circle, as members of the group avoided eye contact with me, and I stood dumbfounded, searching their facial expressions for some kind of clue as to what I had done that had warranted such a frosty reception.

After a few seconds passed, I plucked up the courage and asked, "What's up, guys?"

Silence.

The bell rang signalling the end of break time and just as if I were invisible, the group virtually walked through me, erupting into conversation almost immediately as they broke away. One of the girls looked me up and down as she walked in my direction, another kissed her teeth and muttered under her breath as she passed, "She thinks she's too nice!"

Taken aback, I tried to make sense of what had just happened. My brain went into overdrive trying to process what I had just witnessed.

Was she referring to me? Surely not. Think I was too nice? I didn't even think I had one redeeming feature, let alone class myself as anything remotely close to 'nice'! (attractive).

Shocked and confused, I replayed the events over and over in my head as I sat in R.E. class and could not focus on anything else for the rest of the day.

Being frozen out of the group was a common occurrence for me, but the timing and reasoning never ceased to catch me off guard. Just when I began to think I was finally being accepted by the group, the rug would be pulled out from under me, and I would be reminded that I was dispensable. I would be excommunicated for any number of minor offences ranging from speaking out of turn or vocalising a difference of opinion to generally anything that didn't demonstrate toeing the party-line. All were perceived as acts of defiance and apparently warranted punishment.

Another time the group stopped talking to me for weeks and dismissed me when I attempted to give my input for a dance routine 'we' were choreographing for an upcoming talent show. Following that incident during lunch break, the group cornered me enroute to third period and one of the girls propositioned me. "Do you want to hang out with us?" She asked.

I hesitated, sensing a premeditated set-up. Cautiously, I replied, "Ok, sure."

And then, the unfathomable happened, the most peculiar of ultimatums followed.

The rest of the girls joined the conversation and encircled me, and the same girl replied, "You can hang out with us if you admit that last week when you came to school with your hair in beads, you thought you were pretty!"

I paused, completely perplexed. "No, I didn't!" I replied.

"Just admit it," another girl chimed in.

Stunned, I stood with my mouth wide open, blinking profusely in disbelief, as they moved in closer.

"Just say it," another girl echoed. "You definitely thought you were nice with those beads in your hair!"

I couldn't believe what I was hearing.

"But I really didn't," I protested. Struggling to grasp the reality of the situation and what I was being coerced to confess.

The truth was I didn't think I looked pretty, and I didn't understand why they were so hell-bent on trying to diminish what little self-esteem I had left.

I was always experimenting with my hair and was just finding ways to weigh it down and make it more manageable, it had nothing to do with feeling pretty, but the group were not convinced.

"Ok fine," the first girl snapped before they simultaneously turned and walked away.

I had not given them what they wanted, and the jury had decided, and the verdict was in—my alleged ego needed to be taken down a peg or two—nothing a few days in solitary confinement wouldn't fix!

This time, I decided enough was enough; these girls weren't interested in being friends and they certainly didn't know me if they thought I was conceited. I didn't like how they made me feel and I didn't like myself when I was around them. I felt small, undervalued and belittled. I decided instead of seeking redemption this time, I was going to accept my outcast status and focus on my more nurturing co-existing friendships, away from the group.

However, my decision to function autonomously outside of the confines of the mean girls' collective only served to make things worse.

It was during this time that I first really experienced colourism. As I walked along the corridor to class, they would shout 'Yellow face' and 'Banana girl' in my direction, on account of my fairer complexion. Sometimes their comments were strategically out of earshot, but the inaudible remarks still caught my attention as they were followed up with cackles of laughter and darting looks in my direction.

I took refuge amongst my White friends and my best friend, Mich. But whilst they were sympathetic, they genuinely did not understand why I was being shunned and the concept of colourism was truly lost on them. They also feared the mean girls and wouldn't dream of publicly challenging them in my defence, and quite frankly, I didn't blame them.

In 'secret support', Mich and the others would write me letters filled with affirmations and encouragement that I would read during break time when I was on my own, or as a distraction on my dreaded bus journey home. They would make me friendship bracelets and give me trinkets to lift my spirits whilst 'in exile'. But still, I felt alone.

Every day I dreaded the journey home. At the bus stop, they would employ intimidation tactics to unnerve me, shooting me deadly stares and brushing up against me as they walked past. My heart raced uncontrollably as they approached, pounding in my chest so hard I was convinced it could be heard out loud.

Piling onto the bus when it arrived, I waited until last to avoid confrontation riddled with dread, I followed up the winding staircase, attempting to locate a seat before the bus began its departure and my humiliation was magnified by being tossed to and fro on the upper deck. Sometimes I would walk up to the further bus stop to avoid encountering them and sit downstairs when I got on in hopes of being undetected.

On one occasion when I did this, one of the girls popped her head down the stairwell and locked eyes with me, before disappearing back up the stairs and moments later, in a booming voice, announced to the group, "Yeah, she's down there!"

I gulped.

Other times, I braved the stairs and confined myself to the front quadrant of the bus as they laughed and chatted and sang aloud. I attempted to immerse myself in a letter written to me from Mich, or I'd act as though I couldn't hear them, and attempt to drown them out with the dulcet tones of my favourite RnB group '3T' on full blast on my Walkman.

I tried to keep a brave face, but inside I felt like something was breaking. Maybe it was my heart, or perhaps my spirit, or maybe it was both.

Things at home made life even harder. Sean had moved out to go and live with Dad, leaving just me, Mum and Camille. Once again, Dad had abandoned me, and the all too familiar pang of rejection seeped in and became unbearable.

I couldn't believe given the choice Dad hadn't picked me. It wasn't that I wasn't happy for Sean or even resented him, I just wanted to go too.

Dad had always made me think he couldn't take me with him because of his circumstances—because of the relationships he was in, or because the places he lived in didn't have enough bedrooms. But now, when the opportunity finally presented itself and he moved into a two-bedroom flat in Greenford, he had taken Sean. I couldn't figure it out. He had the chance to finally put all of his promises into action, and instead, he had reneged on them all. I was immediately transported back to when I was six years old, standing at the top of that staircase distraught as I watched him walk out of my life with no hesitation.

My longing to be with Dad only served to drive a greater wedge between Mum and me. Never especially close, my romanticising of Dad created undeniable friction and tension at home, until I eventually felt as though Mum positively hated me. Living in that house felt like hell on earth and the air in our once harmonious eutopia became thick with the resentment and contempt between us. During less tense days, we kept conversation task-focused, only speaking about chores, dinner money, curfews, and babysitting Camille.

Our exchanges were abrupt and hostile. On our worst days, we didn't speak at all. I ate my meals in the kitchen on a stool beside the microwave, whilst Mum and Camille feasted in the dining room.

I felt like Mum and Sean had always been close and I could tell she missed him, and I was convinced that she wished Dad had chosen me to go and live with him as much as I did. After all, Sean was her first child and her only son; he had given her the keys to motherhood and had been there from the very beginning. His very existence was both symbolic and sentimental.

Camille was her heart. She was her perfect baby girl: spirited, bubbly and tough, not emotional and sensitive like me. She was always smiling, her confident, infectious personality was impossible not to love. Mum and Camille spoke in French to each other and had cute little rituals before bed. Tucking her in and closing the door, Mum would serenade, "Bonsoir, mon chéri!"

Camille would then reply from the top bunk of her bed, "Bonsoir, Mama!"

And then, there was me. The middle child. I didn't have a special place or at least I didn't feel like I did with Mum. All the years I had spent following Dad around like a loyal, four-legged friend had caused me to neglect my relationship with my birth-giver and now it felt like she was holding it against me, and it was too late for any kind of reconciliation.

She never came into my room to wish me goodnight. We never hugged or kissed, in fact, I wasn't an affectionate child at all apart from with Dad. He had always kissed and cuddled me growing up and he was the only person that ever told me he loved me. As a result, love and affection became synonymous only within the confines of our relationship and had never spilt over into my parallel relationship with Mum.

Perhaps in Mum's eyes, I was just a difficult teenager. But with first Dad and now Sean gone, the void of affection felt vast, and I couldn't help feeling as though I was being punished. Punishment for Dad's overindulgence and favouritism of me over the years had pushed her further away. She seemed more short-tempered towards me and would often label me as being dramatic or attention-seeking when I expressed emotion. Being labelled felt debilitating and led me to suppress and conceal my feelings and internalise them.

I didn't share at home all that I was going through at school, and I didn't share with friends how bad things were at home. Instead, I wrote letters to an all-seeing, unknown Being and prayed, that was all the solutions I had on reserve in my toolkit.

Going through financial hardships and difficulties at work, Mum often seemed stressed and irritable, and very often it felt that her treatment towards me and the punishment didn't fit the crime. Things were even worse when she would call Dad to come over to discipline me. I was enraged at her for turning Dad against me and I was equally maddened towards him for taking her side. In some cruel, twisted turn of events, the only time they seemed to be amicable towards one another was when they were chastising me.

At age 13, Social Services intervened when I finally confided in a teacher at school and told her everything that was going on at home. Despite her promises not to, she told me she had no choice and had to alert the authorities. I was placed in foster care for a year. When the mean girls questioned me about why I took a different route home from school and who the elderly woman was that I visited, instead of me telling them she was my foster mum, I told them I was part of a community program, and I was her carer. I was ashamed and didn't need them having any voluntary information that they could use as ammo during my next inevitable showdown.

Seeing Sean at school was heartbreaking. He avoided me and seemed to be holding such contempt towards me, which was evident whenever I attempted to approach him and engage in conversation. He was angry but I didn't understand why. It was clear the family wanted nothing to do with me (especially now I was a snitch). Everyone should have been happy, I thought.

They could have a fresh start without me and in turn, I got to exist in a space where there were no more arguments, violence, or pain. Everybody wins, I thought. But my family saw it far differently.

The worst part of being in foster care was my mandated weekly counselling sessions. I hated them. It was the only place Mum and I met regularly. Dad never showed up. It was the worst hour of my life. I had to sit and rehash the worst events of my life, week in and week out, whilst the counsellor insensitively probed and prodded around in the deepest and darkest corners of my memory, posing loaded questions and interjecting with statements that demeaned and undermined my feelings and implied I was exaggerating or making things up.

The devastation of not being believed felt more painful than the events themselves, that I was being asked to recount.

At the end of the 12 months, the social worker filed her judgement and ruled that I be returned home. Upon delivering the news to me in the living room of my foster home, she stood up readying herself to leave and said as she left the room, "Everyone has had to deal with getting beats, you're not special!"

Soon after that, I returned home, and things were worse than before. My year in care was categorised by my parents and extended family who acknowledged it as 'Nicola's episode' and it was often referred to as such. Mum barely spoke to me, and sparks flew more frequently. On weekends at Dad's, he would erupt into an uncontrollable rage at my 'betrayal' and call me crazy and unstable. The violence and the threats intensified, but I had learnt my lesson, so this time, I told no one.

There was no let-up, at home, at school or anywhere. I was trapped and even worse, I had been silenced. No longer channelling my inner Rosa Parks, the only voice I had now was through writing my letters, and the only thing I had left on my list to ask for was to die.

That year should have been a call for celebration as I won the district championship of Watford, competing at age 14, with girls aged 15 and 16 in High Jump. I snagged the gold medal, breaking a record of 1.4 metres and was featured in the local paper. None of my family even knew I was competing let alone had won.

Mum may have seen my medal hanging off the corner of the TV in my bedroom during an infrequent inspection, but she didn't say anything and neither did I. I was on my own and I knew it.

During this time, my letters became more erratic, no longer the perfectionist, with pristine handwriting or eloquent scripted prose. Presentation and structure were no longer a priority as I fell deeper into a pit of despair and my feelings bled out onto the page. Desperation and hopelessness filled the pages of my diary. I no longer wanted to be Mariah Carey or anyone else, and I certainly no longer wanted to be me. I simply didn't want to be here anymore, all I wanted was to be gone.

It was the only solution that gave everyone, including me an out. It was a win-win for everyone. I planned it all out; I would do it tomorrow after school.

The next day was my worst day at school yet, even worse than the day before, but at least tomorrow would be better I told myself. Tomorrow, I would be gone, a distant memory, evaporated like a puff of air that eventually almost never was.

Knowing the house would be empty, I changed out of my uniform and headed back downstairs. Fighting back tears and my hands visibly shaking, I rummaged through the medicine cabinet in the kitchen, beside the stove. I poured out a handful of painkillers into the palm of my hand and swallowed them. Then I calmly unlocked the kitchen door and walked down the path and into the garage at the bottom of the garden. I lay down on the cold, concrete floor in the dark and waited to fade away.

Several hours passed as I lay there, willing it to happen and pleading with God to let me drift into a deep sleep and never wake up. I could see through the hatch window it was dark outside and the streetlight at the end of the road was now on. Mum would have finished work by now I thought. I waited. After what must have been at least another hour, I stood up shivering in just a short-sleeved t-shirt, tracksuit bottoms and bare feet and sobbed.

I was devastated, it hadn't worked, and I was still here. Freezing cold, my breath making clouds of vapour as I breathed out in the sub-zero garage. Lightheaded, and in a daze, I looked out of the small window down the garden towards the house; the lights were on, Mum was home.

With bloodshot eyes and a tear-stained face, I walked back down the garden path and in through the backdoor. Mum was in the kitchen cooking. I mumbled a withdrawn 'Good Evening' as I entered and avoided eye contact. She grunted back words to the same effect, without looking up, as she tended to pots on the fire. I walked past her. She has no idea what I just did, I thought to myself as I climbed the stairs to my room.

However, at that point, I was convinced even if she had known, she wouldn't have cared. I was sick of being called an attention-seeker and a drama queen, and the last thing I wanted was for what I had just done to be used against me, so I said nothing.

I could hear Camille playing in her room as I reached the top of the staircase. My heart thronged with guilt and my brain was overwhelmed as I thought about her ignorant bliss and pure innocence as she giggled and entertained herself with her toys. I walked across the landing, crept into my room and shut the door. Curled up in a ball on my bed, I buried my head in my pillow and cried myself to sleep. I was still here. *Now what was I going to do?*

Camille was the only thing that mattered to me and despite everything else that was going on, being her big sister was the best job in the world, and so I focused on that. Whilst Mum was at one of her many jobs, I would look after Camille on Saturdays. I would take her to the library, sweet shop and then the park, always in that order—it became our weekend ritual, and I felt so mature doing it.

I would encourage her interest in books and urge her to capitalise on the eight-book allowance at our local library, where we would sit for hours on bean bags in the children's section, perusing the shelves for worthy possibilities, not wanting to waste even one selection on an undeserving title.

Then I would take her to the local corner shop where she had a £1 limit to fill a white paper bag with as many sweets as her heart desired. Her staple selection always included a long gelatine snake for the exorbitant cost of 20p, a whopping 20% of her overall budget. But she didn't care, she was adamant the snake was what she wanted and could not be dissuaded. She would insist on saving the head, the juiciest, most flavoursome part of the snake anatomy for Mum—no mafia connotations intended; in fact, very much the opposite, it was an act of adoration.

She missed Mum, just like I had at her age and by saving this cherished souvenir for her was Camille's way of maintaining that bond until they were reunited; this was how she coped with her 'Jo in the window experience'.

Despite my fractured relationship with Mum, I honoured theirs. I vowed to look after the jelly-severed member, wrapping it in tissue and placing it in my pocket for safe keeping for her to present to Mum later, whilst she returned to her sweetie-bag and continued to gorge on her candy-laden treats. After the sweetshop, it was time for the park. That was our real bonding time, and I think I enjoyed it just as much as she did. I would push her on the swings, and she loved my special swing trick, which I would perform every week on cue.

"Higher, higher!" Camille would squeal as I pushed the swing and it ascended higher and higher into the air with every push before I would suddenly grip the swing mid-air, holding it still for a few seconds as Camille would giggle and squeal in excited anticipation before I would without warning suddenly release the seat from my hands, causing the pendulum shaped object to soar through the air with thrilling momentum.

On the slide, I would make a bridge with my legs as she slid down and I would sit in the middle of the seesaw, shifting my weight to and fro. I wanted her to have the best life and I was determined to do my bit. I loved looking after her, washing and styling her hair, inventing games and puzzles for her to complete and following her around the house with Dad's camcorder to film another one of our infamous family home videos. She was my slice of happiness and my new purpose for living.

As a coping mechanism, when I wasn't looking after Camille, I immersed myself in my studies and my passions to block out my reality. It seemed Mum had the same idea when she enrolled me into a Weekend Arts College (WAC) program in Kentish Town. My classes in acting, ballet, street and contemporary dance were a welcome distraction. The teachers were talented and inspiring, and at the end of every term, industry professionals would come and scout for talent agencies.

I loved being good at something that was all mine, and which allowed me to completely switch off from everything else. For the weekends when I was at Dad's, he enrolled me in tap and ballet classes near his flat, and when he learnt of my sporting success, he enquired about coaching for me and one night a week he would take me to Thames Valley Harriers to train in High Jump at their athletic stadium.

From the outside looking in, life for me seemed to be on the up. I had emerged from my 'phase' triumphant. My grades were always good, and I was excelling in all my extra-curricular activities. But behind the scenes, I was falling apart. I felt like a porcelain doll that had been broken into a million pieces and had had all her pieces shoved back together, barely being held together with super glue and masking tape.

Nothing had changed about my world or the people in it. The evidence of former traumatic experiences was still evident by the deep-rooted cracks that manifested internally. I was broken and no one had gotten the memo to handle with care.

I was always just one instance away from falling apart – an unwarranted spanking, a fallout with friends at school, or a nasty taunt from a family member and my world began to implode all over again. I was stuck in a cycle that I couldn't see a way out of and was running out of reserve. Self-harming and desperate for an out, I began to compare myself to other people, neighbours, friends and family members. Maybe the social workers and everyone else were right, maybe it was me, maybe I was the problem.

8

Re-Invention

Inadequacy and shame became the overriding emotions that consistently competed for pole position in my mind and set me off on a downward spiral as I sunk deeper into a depression. I struggled to understand how everyone else seemed to have successfully cracked the code of this thing called life and why I was rendered clueless. It didn't make sense to me how everyone else seemed to be able to assimilate successfully into their own families and why I was malfunctioning and failing miserably.

I just couldn't get over the fact that everyone else appeared so content with the hand life had dealt them and why I had somehow been short-changed.

Whilst my peers seemed to have their whole lives ahead of them, mine felt like it was all but over. It was as if I had gotten into the ring with life and taken an almighty thrashing, and in the faint distance, I could hear the referee's countdown, signalling the small window remaining for me to regain consciousness and rise to my feet. But I lay there, face down to the mat, weak and demoralised, ready to tap out.

And as the bell rang out, signalling my defeat, I could not think of a single reason to get back up. As my eyes closed and the world became a blur, I felt myself fading and then… everything went dark.

The deep-rooted feeling of despair that I felt was hard to equate and even harder to explain, so I gave up trying. With time, I became exceptionally skilled in concealing my internal angst from the world with a bubbly personality and detracting wide smile, that at times almost had me convinced I felt 'normal'. Sometimes I could go hours without a suicidal thought and in the right company, I could forget all about my feelings of emptiness and hopelessness for an entire day.

But once I was alone again, those all too familiar debilitating thoughts began to resurface, like climbing ivy, in the recesses of my mind, slowly creeping up on me, mercilessly sprawling out and multiplying at an increasingly alarming rate until they overpowered and occupied every inch of my consciousness and obstructed my view; no matter where I looked, the long, weaving vines entangled me, rendering me paralysed.

For a few of my closest allies, I pulled back the curtains on the vibrant, radiant canvas I held up to the world and revealed the gloomy, dull, muted reality of my existence. I talked about feeling like an outcast at school and abandoned by my family and lamented about missing my beloved grandads. I expressed how I wished I could be someone different, someone that everyone liked and maybe even loved. I talked about my suicidal thoughts and the compelling desire to fall asleep and never wake up.

Ill-equipped, they did their best to jolt me back to life with good-intentioned reminders of my future potential, talents and achievements. Their attempts to inject positive reinforcement into my bleak and hopeless reality did nothing to shift the burdensome, dark and heavy clouds that hovered overhead, and only further compounded how alone I felt.

Didn't they understand I didn't want to feel like this and that I would change it if I could? If only it was as easy as just shifting my perspective or focusing on being optimistic. Didn't they think if it was that simple, that I would've tried it by now?

I was neck-deep in a sea of turmoil, and it was going to take more than a few positive words of affirmation to save me from drowning.

Nobody understood me or what I was feeling, and I soon deduced that that meant no one was coming, help was not on the way. I was going to have to find a way to escape this mental anguish by myself. I wanted to be better, to feel better, to look better and for the world to accept me. I wanted to be popular and to feel loved and cherished. I was convinced that if I could achieve these things this would be the key, I needed to unlock ultimate happiness.

And so, by virtue of my 14-year-old naivety, I came to the conclusion that the only way to resolve everything was to reinvent myself, starting with a physical transformation. The world had rejected the old version of me and by reinventing myself, I was giving myself a second chance to get it right, or so I thought.

I felt a rush of euphoria as I processed my sudden epiphany, and dare I say it, I became excited. I felt as though I was taking charge of my recovery and that was empowering. I had thrown myself a lifeline and was holding on for dear life. This was my only chance, and I wasn't going to waste it. This time, I would create a new version of me; this time, it would be one the world would love!

I spent my weekends holed up in my room, trying to tame my unruly mane that had attracted so much unwanted taunting. I practised straightening my hair with tongs and hot-combs and attempted to slick down my unruly baby hairs with copious amounts of Dax hair pomade.

I became obsessed with not giving anyone an opportunity to ridicule me and as soon as I detected a hint of external criticism about my appearance, I became obsessed with 'fixing it'.

Swimming class was the first period on a Monday morning, which was far from ideal. It conflicted catastrophically with my weekend marathon of primping and perfecting my coiffure. My efforts, I soon learnt, had all been in vain, when the mean girls made disparaging comments about my post-pool frizzy tresses as they left the locker room in fits of laughter on their way to second period.

Deciding to forfeit history class, I spent an entire hour in front of the changing room mirror, applying every hairstyling tool and product I had to hand, from my backpack onto my head, determined to get my disorderly, shrunken curls under control before break time. After this ordeal, I resolved by forging a sick note, requesting that I be excused from weekly swim class altogether.

Then, after several months of begging, my parents allowed me to get a chemical hair relaxer (a permanent hair-straightening treatment). I had convinced them and myself that my instant makeover would be the answer to all my prayers and signal an end to what they referred to as 'a phase I was going through'!

I was ecstatic as Dad dropped me off after school at the hairdresser's home and drove away. Seated in her dining-room-waiting area, I was overjoyed as I flicked through her collection of hair magazines and marvelled at the fact that completion of my transformation was just a few hours away. It was as if I had won the lottery and was relishing at the prospect of this new life on the horizon and all the things I would soon be able to buy.

In mid-daydream, I was beckoned over to sit in the styling chair, where the stylist mixed up the chemical formula before beginning to apply it to my scalp. The pungent, cold cream substance was not on my scalp for long before it began to sting, sending a burning sensation that pulsated across the entirety of my head.

"Is it stinging?" She asked.

"A little," I winced.

"That's normal." She chuckled as she continued to apply copious amounts of the formula to my head, smoothing it out from root to tip with a tail comb, the motion only serving to intensify the excruciating sensation of my scalp being on fire.

An agonising 60 minutes later, she escorted me upstairs to her bathroom where I sat in a rickety wooden chair with my head tilted back into the sink and waited in pain, with clenched teeth as she guided the shower head across from the bathtub and adjusted the water temperature, twisting and turning the taps left to right.

Desperate for her to saturate my hair with ice-cold water, I waited, squirming around in my seat. I tried to distract myself by counting the specks on the bathroom ceiling and cast my mind back to the age-old adage that had been drummed into the heads of myself and many other little tender-headed Black girls growing up, who had also like me writhed around and squirmed in agony in the beauty salon chair, 'Pain is beauty!'

'Gush'

A cold, soothing blast of water hit my scalp. Relief. As she began to shampoo my hair, I felt a sting on the nape of my neck.

"Ouch," I yelped, sitting up in the chair.

"Your scalp is going to feel sore for a few days," she advised, as she guided my head back towards the sink bowl and continued to scrub.

Back downstairs, the formula now thoroughly washed out, a tingling sensation trickled across my scalp as she applied medium heat and began to blow dry my newly straightened tresses. I was desperate to see if all that pain really had been worth it, the absence of any mirrors on the walls made the anticipation all the more tantalising. It was as if I was part of an extreme makeover, gearing up for the all-encompassing, big reveal.

Although I couldn't see it, I could tell from the ease of her brush strokes that my hair was a lot straighter and lighter in its density. My scalp felt extremely tender as she parted my hair with a wide toothcomb and split it into sections. I tried to blindly calculate the length of my newly straightened tresses as she brushed my hair down my back and tried to catch a sneak peek of my newly acquired texture as she tossed it back and forth with the tongs across my face, before laying each strand with precision along the contour of my shoulders.

I drifted off again into a daydream. I envisioned my new Rapunzel-like locs, swinging to and fro as I walked into school on Monday.

I would enter the playground, walking with a newfound sense of confidence and purpose, past the mean girls as they stood on the sidelines, rendered speechless at my new transformed appearance. They would resign themselves from making any snide comments or quips in my direction and instead, skulk away and retreat in disbelief as my classmates crowded around me cooing and cheering. Just then, my playground crush who had previously barely even noticed that I existed, would now look up and in mid-conversation stop suddenly, as he caught sight of me from across the field and in utter amazement would point in my direction, whilst with the other hand deliver a sharp prod to the ribs of his nearest confidant and enquire, "Who is that!" Real eye-opening, jaw-dropping, diet Coke break vibes; it was going to be great!

"All done!" The hairdresser exclaimed, bringing me back to reality.

She stepped back, facing me, admiring her handiwork before reaching for the vanity mirror on the side.

"Well, do you like it?" She quizzed as she handed the mirror to me.

I held it up and looked. I don't know who I was expecting to see looking back at me in the reflection of the mirror, but I was instantly disappointed to see that I still looked like me.

My hair was longer, straighter, and somehow even a little darker. It looked healthier and more manageable I thought as I examined my neatly coiffured top knot ponytail in the mirror. But I wasn't blown away. My unrealistic expectations seemed miles away from the reality that I could now see, looking back at me.

"I love it!" I lied through gritted teeth.

It wasn't that I didn't like it, I did. It was nice, just not life-changing nice. I had invested so much into this moment, but the suspense and anticipation had all culminated in a disappointing anti-climax. I didn't feel any different, well maybe a little, but not enough that my depression immediately evaporated as I had expected it to, nor enough that I felt like a Disney princess that had been transformed for an infamous ball and looked all new and sparkling.

Sensing my disappointment, she asked, "Are you sure you like it?"

"Yes, yes, I do!" I replied, this time attempting to muster a little more enthusiasm. I smiled as I handed her back the mirror, pulled off my barber gown from around my neck and got up from the styling seat, whilst avoiding making any eye contact.

"Thank you," I said as I handed her the money Dad had given me and followed her to the front door.

Walking to the bus stop to make my way home, I intermittently stopped to look at myself in my pocket mirror. I liked my new hair, but I didn't feel any different. I didn't feel empowered like I promised myself I would. I barely even felt optimistic. Everything felt the same.

In the coming days, I endured a steep learning curve on upkeep and maintenance. My new hair regime was a lot more demanding. My bedtime routine no longer consisted of just installing some haphazard, pillow-worthy plaits moments prior to falling into bed. My new, more fragile, chemically treated mane now needed to be skilfully wrapped before bed—a technique that required much practice and precision, before being secured with a silk or satin headscarf in order to maintain moisture and avoid unwanted friction as I slept.

I had to conduct fortnightly hot oil masks and steam treatments in between washes. The maintenance of my 'new look' was something I had naively overlooked during my pre-transformation fantasies, and quite frankly, I was clueless about how to manage my new textured hair anywhere beyond that pre-empted monumental moment of change. There were no YouTube channels or natural haircare tutorials online back then to help me navigate this new world of chemically processed hair.

Within a year, my hair was severely damaged and much of it fell out due to over processing. I couldn't believe I was losing my hair for the second time.

An emergency trip to the hair salon resulted in ten inches of my damaged-beyond-repair locs being chopped off. I was devastated. So much for a permanent fix; the only thing that seemed to be permanent was my state of depression.

School life had gone from bad to worse. Break times were the most daunting, that's when I was most vulnerable. Without the sanctity of a classroom and a teacher present, I was open to the elements and spent most of my break time trying to avoid the mean girls—those 25 minutes in between lessons felt like an eternity. I felt like a sitting duck, and it was only a matter of time until they would finally encounter me along the corridor en route to class or hiding out in the girls' toilets, and the public humiliation would ensue.

My nerves became so bad I began bunking off from lessons that I shared with some of the mean girls in my year, knowing the rest of the girls would be lying in wait on my exit. Eventually, my anxiety became so debilitating, I couldn't face going to school at all.

It felt so unfair. I was being robbed of the one thing I was good at, and that I enjoyed—learning. My grades in the top set began to plummet as I missed homework assignments and deadlines for projects. I didn't know what to do, I didn't have a plan; all I knew was that I could never go back there.

On the days that followed, I would get dressed and leave for school, wait at the bus stop until Mum had left for work before returning home and letting myself back in. Surprisingly, I quickly assimilated to life outside of education and was able to push thoughts of my traumatic experiences and subsequent failing grades to the back of my mind as I went about my day, sauntering around the house, listening to music, and eating cereal on the sofa whilst watching cartoons.

A few weeks later during the Christmas break, I bottled up the courage to tell Mum about the double life I had been living. Our relationship was far from repaired and I knew how important it was to her that I maintained good grades, which only heightened my anxiety in revealing the truth to her. Apprehensive, I entered into the living room where she was sitting on the sofa, watching TV.

I had no idea what I was going to say, but I knew I couldn't put it off any longer. The new term was just a few weeks away and it was just a matter of time before a letter from the school arrived, notifying her of my unexplainable absence.

"Mum," I stuttered.

She looked up, startled by my sudden presence.

"I haven't been going to school for the last month and I'm not going back there!" I blurted out.

A look of shock washed across her face as I could see her trying to process my unexpected outburst. I stood, holding my breath, and bracing myself for her response. I anticipated her usual empowerment speech to follow, which went along the lines of "Nic, I know it is not easy, but we all have to do things we don't like sometimes," followed by an all too familiar anecdote from when she was a teenager at high school and was treated like an outsider by her peers, but persevered and held her head up high.

But surprisingly, she said nothing. She just stared into my eyes.

The silence was broken as I erupted with emotion and fell onto the sofa beside her and began to relay the events of the past few months. And to my surprise, she just listened, and when I finally got to the end, exhausted and sobbing, she leant over and hugged me and simply replied, "Ok."

I don't know if it was the intensity of my conviction or the fact that it seemed so out of character for me to miss school, that instantly conveyed to her the gravity of the situation, but either way, she did not object. 'Ok' was just one word, but it was like a release valve had gone off in my brain. I felt my entire body go limp and I exhaled. My sorrowful tears turned to tears of relief.

"Ok," she repeated. "We will find somewhere else," she said as she cradled me.

The school search ensued almost immediately, time was of the essence. Mum and I spent hours on the computer conducting searches and Mum had agreed to let me have some input in the final choice this time. I wanted to go somewhere nearer to home and Mum agreed, provided it had good reviews and a well-rounded curriculum.

I started at the new school a couple of weeks into the January term and joined my new classmates in the middle of ninth grade. The head of English showed me and Mum around when we first went to visit. She told me she was impressed with my grades in English and looked forward to teaching me and assured me I wouldn't suffer any bullies there.

Walking back to the car after the tour, Mum and I smiled at one another. "I think you'll be happy here, Nic Nic!" She exclaimed and winked.

"Me too!" I beamed back.

My new school was everything my old school wasn't and that suited me just fine. The racial demographic of the population; teachers and students alike were very diverse. I had a Black form tutor for the first time ever and the environment felt more relaxed, with the right balance of leniency and strictness.

I attracted a lot of attention in the early days as the new girl and was referred to by several admirers as 'the new lighty' on campus. An expression in reference to my fair skin, perceived to be a compliment. I should have been offended by the colourist-loaded epithet, but at the time, I was so weary of jeopardising my newfound popularity and relieved that I was actually attracting positive attention for once, I didn't object.

Mindful not to alienate myself from the outset, I made sure not to get carried away with the novelty attention I was getting by shifting my focus onto making friends. I knew only too well that establishing deep connections with my peers was what would ultimately make or break my integration into my new environment.

The complex structure of the friendships that I built could be broken down into two overarching categories—academic and social—and never did the two mix. I had study buddies I attended class with, we collaborated on group projects and revised for tests together. I shared their enthusiasm for English and Drama, and we enjoyed sharing fiction novels we would later review as a collective.

They understood me and my passion for learning. We had a healthy competitiveness when it came to coursework grades and exam results, and around them, I didn't feel like a know-it-all, a do-gooder or a boff for being a prefect. Unlikely foes, we bonded over our common interests.

The social group, on the other hand, was a co-ed clique of about 15. Most of whom had less interest in academia and were more interested in simply hanging out. During breaks, everyone would congregate in my classroom, and we would sit around listening to music, reading Hip-Hop magazines, laughing and joking and sharing light banter. My former summers with my big cousins had put me in good stead to hold my own with witty retorts and razor-sharp comebacks whenever the spotlight was on me, resulting in me always emerging reasonably unscathed.

It wasn't long before my newfound popularity began to shift both my internal perception as well as external outlook. I realised I was being my true authentic self and was being rewarded for it with widespread acceptance. I was no longer constantly trying to please or shapeshift to fit my environment. I was simply being me, kind, a loyal friend, outspoken, courageous, witty, playful and fun and it was working.

I was well liked and most importantly, I liked who I was becoming. I was evolving. I began to feel confident in my own skin, literally and figuratively. The re-invention seemed almost complete.

Never one to stay in any one social setting for too long, I became somewhat of a social butterfly, flitting from one group to the next. Being confined to just one space just didn't appeal to me and every now and then, I needed a change of scene. Sometimes I craved intellectual stimulation, other times I desired light comedic relief and at other times I needed quiet time alone.

This pattern was indicative of my behaviour even from a young child when after an extended period of interactive play with nursery friends, I would disconnect and go and hide, and sometime later would be found by a teacher, alone, quietly reading a book or drawing. Always unable to explain my sudden disappearance when asked. As a teenager, when visitors would come by the house at some point I would sneak away and could be found in my bedroom, sitting in darkness in deep contemplation, only to emerge an hour later with a renewed injection of energy.

In the early days, I think observers simply thought I was just attention-seeking and in later years, perceived me as a typical temperamental adolescent. A notion that was not helped by the fact that I, myself, could not explain why I would have bursts of high-energy interaction shortly followed by moments of complete withdrawal. It is only as an adult I have come to learn that these are traits of me being an introverted extrovert, someone who needs interaction and solitude in frequent and equal measure, allowing time to recharge and reset.

As a result of my disposition, I regularly switched in and out of my friendship groups at my new school. It was a risky approach, but I stayed true to what felt right for me and that took priority (for a change) – no longer preoccupied or concerned about being ejected for failure to pledge allegiance to one group, as I had experienced with the mean girls. This was the new me and she was fed up with pleasing everyone else but herself.

Fortunately, my approach paid off and my friendship groups seemed unfazed by my unpredictable absences and sporadic reappearances, and always greeted me with warmth and acceptance whenever I came around for break time or hung out after class. I had finally found the right balance and had discovered a sweet spot between being completely myself and fitting in.

The trichotomy of my three best friends each reflected a different dimension of my personality and represented collectively who I was at the very core; sociable yet studious, vocal yet rule-abiding, fun and outgoing yet cautious and self-reflective.

First, there was Gazza, she was my best friend in the top set, and we shared a mutual interest in art and design. She was extremely talented, and I was in no doubt that her artistic talents were far superior to my own, despite her modesty. I was often left in awe at her impressive designs and creative masterpieces. One day in art class, she took my notebook and doodled a design of my fantasy prom dress as I dictated—an asymmetrical, electric blue, Chinese qipao-style dress, complete with Knot Frog buttons, embroidered dragons and muted gold lining.

I was so impressed that a few months later I took the sketch to a dressmaker to 'recreate' for my prom and she couldn't believe it had been designed by a 15-year-old and not an industry professional.

Gazza's pocket-sized stature meant that I towered over her by at least eight inches, making us an odd visual pairing, to say the least, but we didn't care, our bond was deeper than any distracting physicality.

She could certainly be described as feisty and like me, stood up for herself. She was the first friend I had ever had who shared that same Rosa Parks spirit and was not afraid to vocalise her opinion if she witnessed a miscarriage of justice. When our draconian chemistry teacher would single me out and send me out of class unjustifiably, she would go head-to-head with him, calling out his unreasonable actions, often resulting in her being served the same fate. Undeterred, she would emerge from the classroom, where she had been ordered to join me in the corridor, still arguing her case as the teacher hurried her exit from the room by slamming the door behind her. As our eyes met and we realised we were now alone, we would exchange rebellious smiles before erupting into laughter. Gazza always had my back. She was my person, and I was hers.

Then there was Ky. Ky was a ball of fun and energy. Time with her was never dull and in all the lessons I attended with her (which fortunately for the sake of my grades weren't many), I always became distracted, resulting in my exercise books for those lessons remaining relatively empty. We talked about everything: music, family, fashion, boys, nothing was off limits, and yet despite us talking all day and over the phone after school, we never seemed to run out of things to talk about, much to the irritation of our year ten maths teacher.

He would often threaten to split us up to halt our incessant talking, but never followed through, as we humorously pleaded with him offering empty promises to refocus, that we knew we could not fulfil.

Ky was less of a rebel and was more persuasive than she was confrontational, providing far-fetched excuses for missed homework deadlines and comedic one-liners for unexplained absences. She made no secret of the fact that she found school life boring and only seemed to enjoy the excitement that came from any opportunity for anarchy and deviation.

And then there was Jay; he was my male bestie. We hung out in the same co-ed group the majority of the time. We had a playful love-hate rapport. He was like an annoying brother; the first one to roast me on any given day but also the first to come to my defence if any of the guys stepped out of line. He was hilarious, bright, extremely funny, and every bit the class clown. Jay was my rough-house buddy, and we would often playfight and physically taunt each other whenever we met, it was our love language.

Despite our closeness, no one ever questioned if we were more than friends. Our close relationship, although platonic, was evident for all to see. Jay felt like the male version of me, and I felt completely myself around him and no matter how many times we argued and fell out, our tight bond never waned.

Within a few months of my new school, I began dating one of the most popular guys in school; we'll call him 'Highschool Heartthrob'. My social status continued to skyrocket, and school life felt good at last.

High school Heartthrob was the jock type, he went around with the popular crowd. He was really tall, good looking, and wasn't lacking in female admirers. I heard his name come up a few times in the first few weeks of starting at the new school and it had been brought to my attention that he had been making enquiries about me. Yet, it still came as a complete surprise when one break time, he knocked on the girls' toilet door, accompanied by several members of his crew and passed my friend a note to pass on to me, asking me out—so high school!

We squealed and giggled with excitement inside the bathroom, whilst my friends cooed with comments like 'He's so fit!' and 'You two would look so good together', whilst he waited patiently on the other side of the door, probably able to hear the whole debate!

"Yes." I blushed as I stuck my head around the door and our eyes met for the first time. His nervous expression faded and was replaced by a wide smile. Boy, you're handsome, I thought to myself.

Trying to conceal my shaking hands, I wrote out my landline number on the back of his exercise book (pre-mobile phone era) and handed it back to him. He then embraced me, and I completely disappeared inside the padding of his huge puffer jacket. It felt good, I didn't want to let go. He then pulled me away and planted a kiss on my cheek before whispering in my air, "I'll see you later, beautiful."

I felt my heart melt as he walked away. Excited, I ran back into the toilets, greeted by a hero's welcome as my friends whooped and cheered and I fell out smiling and blushing with exhilaration. It was official, I was off the market.

At the end of the school day, I met High school Heartthrob waiting for me at the gates. With my friends in muted silence a few paces ahead, he walked me to the bus stop. I was so nervous, secretly praying that he didn't create a spectacle by leaning in for a kiss as the bus arrived. Fortunately, the moment was avoided, when he offered to accompany me and got on board. As we sat side by side on the top deck, surrounded by our peers, he pulled me close and wrapped his arm around me.

It felt like he wanted to make a statement and mark his territory for any unknowing admirers who frequented my route home that hadn't yet got the memo that we were an item. As the top deck filled up, he was repeatedly greeted by male acquaintances who stopped to not so discreetly examine me before giving him a less than subtle nod of recognition, followed by him returning to them a ceremonious fist bump as they continued to their seats. I felt like a trophy but felt assured that at least that meant he was proud to show me off.

I looked down at my hand, his fingers intertwined with mine. Overwhelmed, I glanced towards the window, catching a glimpse of my reflection in the glass and immediately, I was struck with the stark contrast of just how much my life had changed in just a few months.

The love affair was brief and before long, it was over. Quite out of the blue, he called one evening and after a few minutes of speaking he announced, "Our spark has gone, I think we should end it."

Slightly taken aback, I kept my composure and told him that that was fine, before exchanging goodbyes and hanging up. I then returned to the living room to resume watching *Eastenders*. Despite him breaking up with me, I was surprisingly OK with it. I didn't want anything serious. So, in my mind, it was the best outcome for all involved.

The plan was to just move on. Or at least that is what I intended for us to do, amicably and discreetly. But High school Heartthrob had other ideas.

The day after a breakup in any social setting is pivotal, especially if you and the infamous ex are likely to encounter one another in public. With that in mind, I made sure to look my best. That morning before school, I applied a little extra lip gloss and added a few extra baby waves to the perimeter of my hairline. It was critical to ensure my polished outward appearance effectively offset any suggestions from his friends or mine that I looked downtrodden or worse, heartbroken about being dumped.

Throughout my first lesson, I had a churning knot in my stomach, anticipating the inevitable awkward encounter that was nearing the horizon as we scrambled in between second and first period. Entering the long corridor of B Block, I almost immediately spotted the outline of his tall frame amongst the crowd. He continued to walk towards me from the opposite end of the hall. I held my breath and tried to remain calm, engaging in distracting conversation with friends as we neared one another in an attempt to steady my nerves and shift my focus. This was it.

All eyes were on us as we met in the middle of the corridor, but instead of acknowledging me, he completely blanked me. I was stunned. Trying to conceal the feeling of shock from my face, by my ex's less than amicable disposition, I continued to class.

Throughout second period, I couldn't stop thinking about what had just happened. I felt humiliated and confused. It didn't make sense; what did he have to be mad at me about? Granted I didn't have a lot of relationship experience to go on at this point, but I was pretty sure the dumpee was the one entitled to act as the scorned lover. I hoped that in a few days, things would blow over, and everyone's attention surrounding the fallout between High school Heartthrob, and I would soon become yesterday's news.

But for some strange reason, he seemed insistent on fanning the flames and keeping our tumultuous love affair on the front page, for all to see.

In the coming days, these dreaded encounters intensified, and he soon went from ignoring me to verbal hostilities and mockery whenever our paths would cross. It seemed at one point that he was so hellbent on making my life a misery that he was purposely seeking me out, as he and his friends would shout comments in my direction out of classroom windows and disrupt my sports lessons heckling me from the sidelines. I couldn't make sense of it.

Was he upset that I didn't beg him not to break up with me? Had he hoped I would protest?

It hadn't even crossed my mind to fight for him. As far as I was concerned, if someone wanted to break up, you broke up and that was it.

I hadn't even contemplated that he may have been attempting to call my bluff. But that would have gone some way to explaining his bizarre reaction to a breakup that he initiated.

I did my best to ignore him and his friends, despite how confronting things became. I had dealt with bullies before, and I wasn't about to run away in fear again and lose this new life I had worked so hard to create. This time, I was going to stand my ground. I couldn't let him win; I couldn't let him see me sweat. But just when I thought he had done all he could conceivably do to get a rise out of me, and failed, he played his trump card.

9

Flatline

One of the highlights of the youth social calendar in North West London was the Spring Pinner Fair. All local teenagers descended on the area for the event of the year. The intentions were clear: you went to meet up with friends, go on fairground rides, and showcase your newest name brand street wear in hopes of impressing your secret or not-so-secret crush, who was bound to be in attendance. It was the place to be seen, or it was at least if you were 13–16 years of age and lived in North West London, between Wembley and Harrow!

I remember that day vividly. I was on the Ferris wheel with a friend when, for some reason, I leant forward and looked down into the crowd below and directly beneath me was High school Heartthrob walking hand in hand, laughing and frolicking with one of the mean girls from my old school. Then right on cue, they both glanced up at me and smirked before disappearing into the crowd.

My heart felt like it missed several beats, as my brain scrambled to process what I was seeing.

What was she doing here? How did she find me? And what was she doing with him?

I was speechless as my mind raced with a thousand questions and my emotions became so overpowering, I struggled to breathe. As the ride came to a halt, my friend turned to me and asked me if I was OK; determined not to fall apart right there and then, I told her I felt queasy from the ride and was going to head off home.

As I exited the fair, diverting in-between stalls and down several back roads, to avoid accidentally stumbling upon them, I arrived at the bus stop, my heart racing and my legs visibly shaking, I sat down in utter disbelief. I tried to regulate my haphazard breathing and calm myself down. I felt like a fugitive on the run that had finally come to the end of the line—there was no escape, my past had caught up with me and was threatening to take with it every shred of hope for a new future.

She was going to tell him all about my past, how I was ostracised and humiliated, and the nicknames they taunted me with. I would no longer be perceived as the popular, confident new girl when everyone found out how low the mean girls had placed me on the social totem pole. She could weaponise him with the secrets of my past, and soon history would repeat itself and I would be an outcast again, mocked and ridiculed, with nowhere to run.

As these thoughts flooded my brain, my anxiety evolved into sheer terror and left me teetering on the edge, moments away from a full-blown panic attack in the street. I closed my eyes and repeated my chants aloud, "They can't hurt you; you're going to be OK!" over and over under my breath until I gradually felt my heart rate stabilise and my involuntary shaking cease.

In the coming weeks, I was regularly confronted with the image of the mean girl at my school gates hugging and kissing High school Heartthrob in full view, for all to see. I walked past them and continued to the bus stop. The world was watching (well maybe just the school, but to a 15-year-old, the two were very much the same), and so when it felt like everyone was looking in my direction for a reaction, I did my best to maintain a blank expression and avoid eye contact.

I attempted to block them out, appearing to be engrossed in deep conversation with friends as we boarded the bus. Blocking things out had become somewhat of a speciality of mine. So, whilst burying feelings of betrayal and humiliation, I relied on my tried and tested coping mechanism with fervent determination. After all, there was so much at stake, this was my second chance, and I couldn't give up (again). I heard through the grapevine a few weeks later that they had broken up. I wasn't surprised and by then I didn't care either.

Despite the brief setback, after Highschool Heartthrob left for college and I moved into my final year of high school, things rapidly improved. I had made it to the home straight, I told myself. For a brief period, Mum and I grew closer. I felt indebted to her, and regularly expressed my gratitude for the 'get out of jail free card' she had granted me, in allowing me to leave my old school and forge a new life, and in turn, she was delighted at my newfound zeal for life, resilience and confidence.

The summer of my GCSEs was intense and for the first time in a long time, I felt immense pressure from teachers and family to do well, not to mention the added pressure I put on myself. I was only too aware of how important it was to get good grades, get into a good college, then go onto university and then the career of my dreams to finally achieve ultimate eutopia. I had it all mapped out and had come to the conclusion that this was the only way I could guarantee the life I had always wanted, but it all hinged on this very season, and I couldn't mess it up. My life depended on it!

Week after week, I spent every spare minute I had after school and on weekends in my bedroom revising. During study leave on any given day, I could be found sitting at my collapsible desk in my room, with my head in a book. Scrawling through notes and annotating textbooks became my daily ritual and before I even realised, spring had turned into summer.

During momentary breaks from studying in my room, I would walk over to the window and peer out, distracted by the sound of the older kids in the neighbourhood convening in the front garden of the house across the street, playing music and chilling in the summer sun. As feelings of FOMO (fear of missing out) began to set in, I watched with envy, before reluctantly tearing myself away from the window with self-promises that once my exams were over, I was going to have the best summer ever.

Day and night, I recited my colour-coded cue cards until I could see the words etched in my brain and knew the colours and corresponding script by heart. It was tough but I got great satisfaction from feeling that I was actively bettering myself and etching that little bit closer to my designer future life.

Whilst taking my exams and revising, things at home had become strained. Mum and I had discontinued counselling, despite not working through several unresolved issues, and over time, a deep-seated resentment between us began to manifest and caused our communication to almost completely break down. My relentless revision schedule became a welcome distraction from the tense atmosphere at home.

Then randomly one day, Mum called me downstairs. As I descended the stairs and headed towards the dining room, I heard a man's voice and realised Dad was there. When I entered the room, they told me to take a seat and proceeded to tell me that they were introducing a new rule—a one-hour bedroom ban. Dad went on to explain that for one hour a day, I was barred from entering my bedroom and hence revising. I was livid! I couldn't understand why they were conspiring against me and were threatening to destroy all I had been working towards.

If this was their idea of support, it sure didn't feel like it. Excluding me from my room and forcing me to spend time in an already tense environment felt like a punishment. Maybe if they had prefaced the new rule with expressions of concern that I was studying too hard or had suggested some family activity we could partake in together, I would have been more agreeable, but this felt like less of an act of compassion and more an act of control.

The fact that once again Mum had enlisted the help of Dad to come into our home and lay down the law only enraged me further and served to broaden our already widening rift. By the end of summer, things had become unbearable and soon after my final exam, Mum kicked me out.

I turned up at the council housing office with just the clothes I stood in, and all my worldly possessions packed into one laundry bag. My hair was a mess, my clothes dishevelled and unironed, and my eyes puffy and red from crying. Sitting in the council house waiting room, I felt demoralised and ashamed, my eyes remained glued to the constantly revolving entrance doors, mortified at the thought that someone who recognised me would walk in and I would have to divulge the entire ordeal that had led to this point.

I took a ticket and waited to be called to the front desk, contemplating what I would say when I got up there.

Where would I start? How would I answer the simple question of why are you here? That question alone required a multitude of interwoven explanations; because my dad abandoned me. Or because my mum doesn't love me anymore and rejected me. Or because I was too mouthy, too bold, too insecure, too weak, or because I complied with the authorities and went into care, or simply because I was unlucky in life!

For an entire day, I was passed from pillar to post from one council department to another like unwanted trash. From Housing to Social Services to Children's Social Services and back to Housing again, I traipsed along Wembley High Street, with my laundry bag to and fro, between buildings. Back and forth I went, filling out copious documents and retelling my story over and over again. Emotional and desperate, I was forced to repeat that I was alone, that no one wanted me and that I had nowhere else to go.

When the social worker finally returned to the room and announced she had good news and proceeded to tell me that she had been able to allocate me emergency housing, my heart leapt with joy momentarily, only to feel it break and shatter immediately afterwards. She went on to explain that the only reason she had been able to secure accommodation for me was because she had spoken to both of my parents, and they had confirmed that they were relinquishing all parental ties to me and that I was officially estranged.

It all seemed to be happening so fast and before I knew it, she was handing me my paperwork and directing me to the location of the local hostel, and said, "It's a good thing you are now estranged." She smiled reassuringly as she ushered me out of her office and out of the building. It was like a final punch to the gut. Dazed, I stumbled onto the street. Estranged? There was nothing good about it. I had always felt I was alone, but now I had the paperwork to prove it.

30 minutes later, I arrived at the allocated emergency housing, a grotty five-storey hostel in an undesirable part of town. The building was old and dingy. There was no lift, just a narrow, winding staircase, that seemed to go on forever. I climbed to the third floor and attempted to find my room. I walked past the communal kitchen; it was filthy and stunk of fried food and rotting garbage. The stench was permanently trapped in the room by the sealed, stained, watermarked windows, that looked out onto a busy, noisy high street below.

The co-ed bathroom next door was small and pokey, and the shower cubicle was discoloured and covered in wall-to-wall hair. I recoiled in disgust and as I stepped back into the hallway, I noticed my room to the left of the landing. Once inside, I realised it was surprisingly a good size. But the brickwork was dirty, the large Victorian window looked like it had never been cleaned and the wall beside the bed was covered with undistinguishable stains and smears.

To enter and exit the building, you had to sign in and out. The reception was manned around the clock and every time you left, you had to hand your key in. I met Steve, the hostel manager, on my first day. A friendly, good-looking guy who introduced himself as I completed my details in the signing-in book. He had beautiful big brown eyes and wore stylish, designer clothes and name brand trainers.

As the days went by, I became less self-conscious around him. Seemingly unfazed by my present predicament and living arrangement, he always attempted to engage in conversation with me or pass me a compliment as I came and went. He never seemed to run out of things to say and had a warm intensity when he spoke to me, never breaking eye contact. He made me feel like I had value and that I was seen.

I attended the local internet café, looking for jobs and filling out applications online. Steve offered to let me print copies of my CV out in his office and said if I wanted to stay with friends a few nights a week, he would bend the rules and sign in for me.

I stayed at the emergency hostel for around a week before the council moved me to semi-permanent boarding. I thanked Steve for everything and vowed to stay in touch. By the time I received my glowing GCSE results a few weeks later, I was living in a hostel, housed alongside asylum-seeking families. I was completely cut off and isolated. I had finally achieved the first step of my life plan and had aced my exam results (which included several A*s and As), but now had no one to celebrate this amazing milestone with.

I was scared and penniless. I survived on pot noodles and crisp and proceeded to lose close to a stone in a little over two weeks. I hadn't noticed my drastic weight loss until a friend raised concern about my shrinking frame and protruding decolletage.

In less than a month, my whole life had changed. One minute I was leaving school, excited about the prospect of having the world at my feet, and the next, I felt as though it was resting entirely on my narrow, 16-year-old shoulders.

Desperate to retain some form of income and normality, I continued working part-time at my longstanding weekend job. No one at work knew about my homelife and the reality of my situation. And for a few hours a week, I got to escape it too.

When teachers and school friends greeted me at the end of school prom dance weeks later, they were none the wiser of the recent change in my living arrangements and the new trajectory my life was on. I blocked it out, and that night, I partied the night away, and for a few hours on the party boat and amongst old friends, I was able to forget all about the harsh realities of my existence.

The next day, I discovered my exam certificates had been stolen from my room. Despite there being no sign of forced entry, after presenting my compelling case at the front desk, it soon became apparent that they did not intend on investigating the matter further and that the likelihood of getting them back was slim to none. And so, I had to accept that they were gone for good and come up with a plan B. Coming up with a plan B was becoming a regular occurrence in my life, although at times, it felt like I had lapped the whole alphabet several times over.

I walked back to my room and felt the panic begin to set in as I fixated on the knock-on effect of my most recent dilemma. College enrolment was just weeks away. When I called the administration office, I was informed that they would not be able to enrol me or hold my place if I couldn't provide proof of my certificates by the enrolment deadline.

I felt sick to my stomach. This was my chance at getting my life back on track, this was what I had worked so hard for, I had put in the effort and got the grades, and now in the blink of an eye, it was all slipping away from me.

With next to no money and no internet, I took my childhood library card and walked to the local library, hoping that my card would still work and hadn't expired and that I wouldn't be required to provide proof of address, as I was still registered at Mum's. As the light turned green and the barriers at the entrance opened and granted me access, I let out a light sigh of relief, proceeding to the computer counter.

There, in front of a computer screen, I spent hours trawling websites of exam boards and accreditation bodies, sending emails to admissions boards and college deans and visiting college enrolment chatrooms and forums for advice. Every day, I returned to the library to check my emails and to see if there was an update on my appeal to have copies of my certificates issued.

Impatient, I would ring and ask for a status report and was repeatedly reminded of the fact that duplicate copies were distributed at the examining board's discretion and that there was no guarantee that my appeal would be approved. So, I waited, and I prayed, and I tried not to fall apart in the meantime.

Then whilst leaving the library one day, I was unexpectedly confronted by the mean girls. I was completely caught off guard as they came running towards me from across the street. One of the ringleaders began swearing and threatening me as the others encircled me, accusing me of spreading rumours about her and challenging me to a fight. I felt like a lonesome deer, surrounded by a bunch of hyenas with no way out.

Just when I was convinced a beat down was imminent, my aunt pulled up and stopped her car in the middle of the street and ran to my aid. Confronting my bullies, shouting and warning them off, the mean girls quickly retreated and fled as she beckoned me to get into the car. A wave of relief washed over me as she accompanied me back to the hostel.

I wish I had known then that that would be the last time I would ever see them all again, I would have felt much more at ease in the weeks that followed. Needless to say, I never returned to the library.

The only silver lining that summer was a family wedding. At first, I was dreading seeing Mum and my relatives now that I was legally estranged. But unlike before when I was in care, this time it seemed different. This time the feeling of being shunned was replaced by a sense of comradery, at least by my older brother and my cousins as they pulled up in convoy on the forecourt of the hostel to escort me to the main event.

Although no one talked about it, there was a feeling that this time, they sympathised with my predicament, their demeanours less hostile and defensive, the atmosphere more welcoming and the energy felt lighter. Perhaps pulling up to the reality of my situation was evidence enough that my dire predicament could not be entirely self-inflicted, as they had been previously led to believe.

As the August sun beamed down on us, we drove to the soundtrack of Tupac and Biggie Smalls, chiming in for our favourite rap bars or all too familiar chorus, as we cruised to the venue. I suddenly had a flashback of summers past, the feeling of warm nostalgia rushed over me and as the sun beamed through the window, warmly hitting my face, I momentarily closed my eyes. I felt my worries melt away as the rays of sunshine pierced the glass, bouncing off of my cream linen pantsuit, and for a moment, I didn't have a care in the world.

For the first time in a long time, I felt free and safe, and like I belonged. I wanted that car ride to last forever.

A few days later, I received the news I had been hoping for—the exam board had agreed to send out duplicates of my certificates. Too late now to enrol at my first-choice college (where all my classmates were attending), I sprang into action, sending out late applications and attending late admissions open days. Fortunately, one week later, I was offered a place in a college in the heart of Maida Vale, West London.

On my 17th birthday, one week after the term had started, I embarked on my first day of college. Outside my first English lesson, my no-nonsense English tutor intercepted me in the doorway of the classroom as I attempted to enter, and with a stern gaze and undeniable intensity leant in and said, "If it wasn't for your good grades young lady, you wouldn't be here, this class is full!"

I couldn't tell if it was a compliment or a warning, perhaps a mix of both. Either way, I took my cue and attempted to assure her that I was grateful to be there and pledged not to let her down.

Despite being excited about the prospect of finally being in college and potentially having at least one foot back on the road to recovery, it was the worst birthday I had ever had. It was my first birthday where I wasn't surrounded by the familiar faces of friends and family and had some type of event or celebration planned. I wasn't inundated like I was used to with congratulatory cards and phone calls. Even my birthday in care was better than this, I thought. I had never felt more alone.

Reflecting back over the summer that I'd had, it was nothing like what I had envisaged just a few months ago back in my bedroom by the window. Now estranged from my family, living in temporary accommodation, battling challenge after challenge, whilst trying to hold down a part-time job and now studying full time too was overwhelming, to say the least!

All I knew was all I had ever known and believed and that was that education was my only way out—college would lead to uni, uni would lead to an amazing career, and that career would lead to the perfect life at the end of the rainbow. But I was drained. With so much at stake, the pressure sent me into a destructive cycle of suppressing my emotions, hiding my past, and putting on a front with everyone around me: work colleagues, teachers and new friends.

Keeping up the pretence was overwhelming, and I felt like I was swimming like an elegant swan on the surface whilst paddling like crazy under the surface just to keep from drowning. I was barely hanging in there, clutching onto the hope that things would get better, despite how bleak everything looked around me.

I willed myself not to break or to let my thoughts and emotions get the better of me. For all intents and purposes, I was living a double life and concealing my real, broken, damaged state of affairs and frame of mind became a full-time job. The only time I allowed myself to cry was when I got home while writing in my journal. It was my only permitted time of release, and so in the privacy of my room, I cried. As my tears streamed down my face and soaked the pages, for an hour I allowed myself to let go.

Never letting go completely, fearful that letting go completely would send me back into a dark, destructive place that I was too broken and ill-equipped to make it back from. So, I released just enough to let go of the events of the day, leaving just enough resolve for what lay ahead tomorrow. That was my ritual.

As time went on, I began to embrace my new fabricated life and it wasn't long before I was able to immerse myself in it completely. It became an art form as I would shift back and forth between each dimension of my compartmentalised reality. I didn't have a long-term plan but for now, this was working for me and that was all that mattered. Functioning in this way allowed me to fully immerse myself in college life and before long, I was really enjoying it. I had a large group of friends, I enjoyed most of my subjects and for the second time, to my surprise, I had an influx of admirers.

It was at college that I was given the nickname 'Bambi' by an admirer in my media studies class. After flirting for weeks, one day he pulled me aside after class and holding my hand, he said, "You're beautiful, has anyone ever told you, you look like Bambi?" I was speechless. I didn't know what he was going to say, but I certainly hadn't expected that.

Needless to say, I assured him that he was the first, but graciously thanked him for the compliment, knowing that he had intended it as such. He walked me to the station and as we embraced and said our goodbyes, I couldn't bring myself to burst his bubble and tell him that Bambi was actually a boy!

In the coming weeks, his attendance in class dropped and so did my interest. Soon after I found out that he had a girlfriend and a toddler at home—go figure, who else was watching *Bambi* at 17 years old, in college? I thought! I deleted his number but my nickname on campus stuck, and over time I grew to embrace it.

When my temporary tenancy ended at the hostel, I was out. With no means to get accommodation of my own and with no fixed abode, I sofa-surfed in the homes of friends and family for months. For ages, I lived out of black bags, fatigued by the monotony of unpacking and repacking whenever I had outstayed my welcome and it was time to move on.

When some older friends of the family invited me to go and live with them, I was overjoyed and felt like things in my life were finally coming together. I still wasn't in contact with my parents, but I had gained two big sisters in the interim. I had always wanted a big sister and now I had two.

At their place, I had my own room, and could finally unpack my wretched black bags. The location was ideal for my weekend job and only a few stops on the train from college; it felt perfect.

Things started well. The 'big sisters' were always on hand to talk and to give me advice on anything from family to life, to fashion, and would give me makeovers and style my hair. They kept me entertained with X-rated stories about their dating experiences and offered relationship advice like two wise gurus who had lived and seen it all. I looked forward to coming home from college and hanging out in their bedroom every evening, listening to music and watching movies, whilst gorging on takeout; it was like a 24-hour slumber party.

For the first time in a long time, I felt looked after. On regular shopping trips or nights out, they would treat me and pick up the tab. They were generous on account of my limited budget and I in turn expressed my eternal gratitude.

But gradually things began to change, and I noticed how overbearing they became. It was as if I was more like their possession than their little sister. They often resorted to bossing me around and overriding my personal choices. They would belittle me and embarrass me in the presence of their male company and try to control my comings and goings and who I did and did not talk to, treating me more like a seven-year-old than someone burgeoning on adulthood.

When I eventually spoke up and told them that I was not a child and that there were only six years between us, they told me I was being disrespectful and proceeded to bar me from their room. For days, they ignored me around the house and subjected me to the silent treatment, slamming their adjacent bedroom door shut as I ascended the stairs.

Entering into my room, disheartened, in an instant I felt like I had been catapulted back in time and I was being iced out by a group of mean girls again. Only this time, it wasn't as simple, these mean girls held all the power, they could determine my entire fate and they knew it. Once confident to help myself to food in the fridge or take long hot baths in the evening, I no longer felt comfortable when they would encounter me in the kitchen or on the landing on the way to the bathroom.

I no longer felt welcome. I no longer felt like this was my home. I felt unwanted, exposed, and yes, that old chestnut, alone!

As I sat on my bed, I cried, no longer capable of applying my usual emotional restraint, I let it all out and I imploded. I thought how abnormal I must be to not be able to maintain relationships of any kind. I thought about how my family had rejected me and not come to my rescue for the second time. I thought about all the bullying and the taunting and the name-calling I had endured right from being called plunger lips to the week prior when the big sisters had called me a stupid fool.

I thought about the heartache of all my childhood traumas. I thought about my parents, I thought about them abandoning me. I thought about the abuse. I thought about the relentless cycle of challenge after challenge that I had to face whilst friends got to live out the final year of their childhood in ignorant bliss. I thought about everything and everyone I missed. I thought about my grandads, I thought about my sister and if she was asking Mum where I was and when I was coming back to take her to the sweetshop.

I thought about how undesirable my life was and how humiliated I would feel if my current existence played out on the big screen for all my colleagues and college friends to see. I felt ashamed of my ugly reality and the facade that disguised the true unpresentable state of my life. I was embarrassed, I was humiliated, I was a loser. I thought about getting out once and for all, and then I could think of nothing else. And so there in my room, I took a packet of tablets from my rucksack and attempted to swallow them all.

'… Beep, beep, beep'.

I woke up, freezing cold in a hospital bed, in just my socks, a t-shirt and a hospital gown. My eyes—were puffy and swollen, as I attempted to prise them open and establish my surroundings; the fluorescent lights above my head were blinding and my eyes stung and squinted as I attempted to focus. I looked around, nurses and doctors were pacing the corridors, busy, attending to the sick and the needy.

I sat there invisible and ignored, except this time, I wanted it, I deserved it. I was neither sick nor needy, or maybe I was both. I was embarrassed and disgusted. I couldn't even make eye contact with the nurse who routinely stopped to read my chart and check my vitals.

I felt guilty that I didn't feel a rush of euphoria, realising that God had given me another chance, instead all I felt was utter despair and fixated on the nagging question in my mind, why was I still here? I cried uncontrollably like I was grieving, devastated I had survived. I was still here and that meant not only had my problems not gone away, but now they had multiplied, and I had to face the consequences of my actions too. I hadn't planned for this, for once, I hadn't made a plan B.

I looked around my cubicle; it was bare, apart from a chair in the corner of the room which had a pair of my jeans cradled in the seat, no shoes, no purse, no phone. That was it. As I lay in the hospital bed, memories began to flash through my mind of earlier that night. I remembered being loaded into the ambulance as I slipped in and out of consciousness.

I remember a medic repeating my name and in the distance from the street, I could hear the big sisters shouting, "You're on your own now", "You are out!", "Don't come back here!" As it all came back to me, there in that hospital bed, I cried until I had no tears left.

I pushed myself off of the bed and walked into the bathroom cubicle. I stood and examined myself in the mirror, disgusted by the image that looked back at me: my hair in disarray, my tear-stained face and bloodshot eyes. I looked every bit how I felt, a mess! I splashed my face with cold water, my eyes stung, and my skin felt tight. Aching, I attempted to slick down my hair before bending down and pulling on my trousers.

I had no phone, no money, not even a coat. My stomach groaned, sending sharp, lightning pulses up my back. I walked out of my cubicle, along the ward and out past the deserted waiting room and closed gift shop. I looked up at the big clock on the wall, it was midnight. I crossed the beige linoleum floor towards the pay phone, suspended in the corner on a wall. As I walked towards it, I was trying to formulate a plan.

I didn't know any phone numbers without my phone, apart from Mum and Dad's. And there was no way I was calling them; well maybe Dad, I contemplated, but I had no money and no clue how to make a reverse call or even call the operator. I lifted the receiver and began trying to recall Dad's number in my head when suddenly a sound interrupted my thoughts, someone was calling my name. For a split second, I thought I was hallucinating. In confusion and shock, I spun around and there in the empty waiting room like a mirage of hope, stood my dad.

My mouth fell open and before I could say a word, he let out a sigh of relief and cried, "Baby!" I immediately fell to the ground, sobbing uncontrollably. He ran towards me and scooped me up in his arms, and at that moment, it was like I was a little girl again and once again he had come to my rescue. "We're going home," he whispered in my ear. I clung to his arm as I clambered to my feet, and we walked towards the nurses' station.

Everything was going to be OK. And for a while, it was.

10
Love Like This Before

I lived with Dad and his girlfriend and my half-brother in East London for almost two years. It was my first permanent address in a long time.

The arrangement was far from ideal—living on the other side of London, commuting over an hour to work and college every day, being away from everything and everyone I knew and having to share a bedroom with my baby brother, who was ten years my junior.

I found it strange adjusting to life, living with Dad. After pining for years for the opportunity, the reality was nothing like I had imagined. It didn't match the fantasy I'd had at age seven when he visited me in the middle of the night and I pleaded with him to take me with him, or at age 14 when he chose Sean instead of me. It was different, our dynamic had shifted, no longer a dependent minor, I no longer idolised him, now on the brink of adulthood.

It often felt as though I was more of a tenant than living with actual family. Everyone did their own thing, coming and going throughout the day with little interaction or cohesion; in the evenings everyone was in a different corner of the house and at mealtimes, I pretty much fended for myself. It never truly felt like home and from time to time, I felt like my dad's girlfriend saw me as more of an inconvenience than a welcome addition to the family.

Mum and I were finally on speaking terms for the first time in almost six months and I spent weekends at her house, where I could devote time to Camille and was only five minutes away from my part-time retail job.

Despite all that had gone on at my former home and how strange it felt to be back in my old bedroom, this time as a guest, it still felt more homely than at Dad's. Even if at Mum's we were just watching a movie on the couch together or eating Sunday dinner at the dining table, it felt warm and familiar. I looked forward to weekends to be back in my old stomping ground. I could come and go as I pleased unbeholden to Mum, no longer my custodian and out of the watchful eye of Dad. It was the perfect balance of freedom and security.

Living with Dad was not all bad and I cherished the unpredictable moments of spontaneous fun that we shared, often when it was just the two of us. We'd watch old VHS tapes of comedy shows like *Fawlty Towers* and *Only Fools and Horses*, and we would bond over comedy skits and hilarious punchlines. I observed the artform of comedic timing, sarcasm and irony, and learnt to appreciate the skill and craftsmanship of talented comedy writing, an interest that had been sparked whilst watching comedy shows with my grandad on his bed almost a decade prior.

I would watch Dad with intense enjoyment as he would fling back his head and guffaw, whilst slapping his thigh in elation. I deduced that comedy was escapism and I loved how it made me feel and the bond it created between us through our shared comedic appreciation. Sometimes, we didn't stay in and watch a movie, instead, Dad would surprise me and take me out to eat or to the cinema. He always chose the restaurant or the movie we would see, but I wasn't fussed if it meant we got to spend time together.

I also loved being a big sister to my baby brother, Aaron. He was super cute with big brown eyes and the longest eyelashes I'd ever seen on a boy. I remember one day I walked into his bedroom and caught him trying to cut them with a pair of scissors because he said all the girls in class kept calling him pretty. I of course stopped him and promised him one day he would thank me for it!

On some weekends, Camille would come and stay too. They were the best times, watching the two of them play and laugh together without a care in the world, just how kids should be, uninhibited, full of innocence and confidence, it was heart-warming to see. They reminded me so much of me and Sean at that age.

Before long, it had been almost a year since I had been living at Dad's and as my first year of college drew to a close and my favourite month of summer rolled around, I was full of optimism and hope. My studies were going well, I had a large group of friends and I had fallen head over heels in love.

First Love (we'll call him) was the best thing to happen to my summer and the feeling of falling in love felt every bit as magical as is depicted in the classic Hollywood rom-coms I was so infatuated with. Starting out as friends, we connected over our shared interests and bonded over our spirituality and passion for street dance. He was strikingly handsome, and a bit of a show-off—he rode a motorbike and would often walk into college to meet me clad from head to toe in his bike leathers and helmet in hand.

But underneath his hot boy image, he had a kind heart and a gentle soul. He was funny, but sensitive and open, he was a great communicator and demonstrated a vulnerability I'd never experienced in a guy before, let alone a partner. He was a couple of years older than me, but he never made me feel naive in my views or patronised me. He was affectionate and loving and made me feel like I was the most beautiful woman in any room.

We would sit and talk for hours in the common room about the Bible and our life experiences and wouldn't even realise the time until the campus security guard approached us and told us he was locking up the building for the night. On Saturdays, I would tell Dad I was at Mum's and tell Mum I was at Dad's and go to visit First Love at the home he shared with his mum on a busy street in West London.

I would take the train to the nearest stop, and he would come and meet me. Waiting in anticipation for his arrival, my nerves would transform into butterflies as he appeared on the station forecourt and passionately embraced me.

First Love and I would sit in his room talking, playing computer games, and watching videos of breakdance tournaments all day. Suddenly, realising it was dark outside, he would rush me to the station placing a kiss on my forehead, before I descended the stairs in a flurry, just in time to catch the last train home.

A few weeks before the new term rolled around, First Love informed me that he had not done well on his exams and needed to put our love affair on hold so that he could buckle down and complete his retakes. I was crushed.

On a scorching summer's day, around the corner from the college building, he asked me, "Do you believe I will come back for you?"

Slightly miffed by this overly romanticised question, I replied, "I hope so," looking downcast.

His face became crestfallen at my less-than-enthusiastic demonstration of faith. He grabbed me passionately, pulled me in towards him, looked intensely into my eyes, and said, "Babe, make that hope so a know-so."

I focused on revising and rehearsing for my mid-term theatre production and before I knew it, exams were all complete and college was over for the summer. I didn't hear from First Love for three months until out of the blue he turned up and surprised me at the end of September at a nightclub where I was celebrating my 18th birthday. He behaved like no time had passed at all, and I was totally perplexed when he began affectionately hugging and kissing me in every picture I posed for with friends.

My distant demeanour coupled with his smothering tactile behaviour, caused friends and family members to question if we were back together.

"No!" I protested.

We had gone from speaking ten times a day to complete radio silence and I had spent the rest of the summer heartbroken and feeling in limbo trying to repair the void he had left. Getting over First Love was one of the hardest things I'd had to do, and I couldn't go back, it was over. It was clear he wanted to pick back up right where we had left off, but I didn't feel the same way anymore. I couldn't trust him, I couldn't risk him hurting me again. A few weeks later, I heard he was in a new relationship and my heart broke all over again.

One night, my dad's girlfriend came into the back living room where I was sitting in darkness and begged me to stop playing *Boyz II Men – End of the Road* on repeat. As I lamented that I would never love again, she attempted to cheer me up, vowing that I would and that one day she would remind me of this conversation and I would laugh about it—years later, she did, and I did!

My second year of college soon came around. I felt different, post-First Love. I was 18, finally officially an adult. I had passed my driving test and Dad had bought me a pre-loved J reg Ford Escort. The colour wasn't my first choice, and the paintwork was patchy in places, but it was mine and I loved it! I couldn't stop squealing with excitement as Dad tried to get me to focus as he propped up the bonnet and attempted to take me through all the maintenance essentials: checking the oil and water levels and demonstrating how to change a tyre. But I was far too excited to take it all in.

I was the envy of all my classmates and took great pride in being the first of my friends to have a licence and own a car. Ferrying them around for unnecessary trips to nearby food outlets and station drop-offs, I felt every bit the grown-up, and worlds away from the 16-year-old that had left school just two years prior.

Being a new driver, driving over 15 miles a day from East to West London, it was inevitable that eventually I would discover that I wasn't as competent as I had thought, and my driving confidence took a hit along with my new car when I had my first fender-bender. In typical dad style, he rushed to the scene and reassured a distraught me that it was just a scratch and kept telling me not to worry and that metal could be replaced.

I thought he would be disappointed or irritated, but he was surprisingly laid back as he walked me to a nearby auto parts shop before making a few purchases and returning to the car, replacing the headlight and spraining the bumper back into place with his bare hands.

The winter after my 18th birthday, my aunt invited me to a new church in Finchley that she was planning on visiting. I was somewhat surprised at her sudden interest in her spirituality, something I had only ever associated with my mum's side of the family. Growing up, I had had a pretty consistent upbringing in the church, living with my grandparents we were taught from an early age about the Bible and attended church like clockwork.

In my teens, I attended my uncle's church where he was head pastor, and my family made up at least 40% of the congregation. As a result, I felt smothered a lot of the time in that environment and was conflicted by feelings of not being able to express myself freely, constantly under the watchful gaze of my relatives who occupied the front three rows. Eventually, over the years, I went less and less and drifted away from the church, and eventually from God entirely.

But I agreed to go with my aunt, mainly for moral support and partially out of intrigue. I met my aunt at 6.30 pm in the buzzing foyer of an expansive church building filled to the brim with evangelical parishioners who greeted us warmly before we were escorted by an usher into the overflowing grand auditorium.

As he climbed the steep staircase, we followed suit, darting back and forth expressions of amazement to one another, in awe at the sheer scale of the hall and the vast amount of people within it, packed in row after row after row. As he spotted two empty seats up in the rafters, he abandoned his ascent and waved us on.

The atmosphere inside the hall was electric, and the buzz of anticipation filled the air like the excitement inside a theatre before the curtain is about to go up. Then, without warning it started. The praise and worship team began to sing, and the musicians began to play, and a sweet sound began to emit from the stage that started to resonate throughout my entire body. I was overcome, unable to immediately process what was happening.

I suddenly felt self-conscious and vulnerable as I became overwhelmed with emotion standing there next to my aunt and attempted to blot the tears discreetly from my eyes (our family didn't get emotional, it's just not what we did). Not wanting to make things awkward between us or to let the side down by embarrassing my aunt, I desperately tried to mask any evidence of the flood of emotions that were ebbing through me. When I glanced over to her, to make sure my tears had gone undetected, I realised that she, quite uncharacteristically, was overcome too.

This wasn't just good music; I'd grown up all of my life listening to good music and appreciating the soulful ballads of talented vocalists like Whitney Houston, Mariah Carey, and Celine Dion. This was more than a well-executed production or the work of a musical maestro, this was deeper than that, this feeling was coming from within me, and at that moment, I felt an undeniable, transformative shift.

Later in the service when the speaker asked if anyone wanted a change in their life and for that change to be Jesus, I put my hand up and before I knew it, I was walking down ten flights of stairs towards the stage, to accept the invitation for prayer. Tears streamed down my face, I was exposed and in full view of a congregation of over 500 strangers and my aunt, but I didn't care.

At that moment, I felt safe and assured. I felt an indescribable sense of peace wash over me. It was like I had finally accepted the help of a trusted friend who had been there all along, cheering me on from the sidelines, willing and waiting for an invitation to lend a hand. He loved me, He had always loved me, and His love was unconditional, flaws and all.

After that day, even as sceptical as I was, I had to admit, despite how cookie it might sound, that I was never the same again. I felt a new kind of completeness. And for the first time ever, I knew like I knew, that I would never again feel alone. This was my third awakening.

I was touched by the encouragement from family and friends when I shared my news with them. Even my dad, who claimed to be a staunch atheist, was supportive. And I was even further enthused when I told him I had joined a church and had successfully auditioned for the dance ministry. On performance days, he would text me words of encouragement and follow up with phone calls afterwards to enquire how it went.

The following summer, I got baptised. It was a moving, life-affirming experience, and the final stage of my reinvention. I was liberated.

On the day of my baptism, relatives from both sides of the family turned up in support. It was a beautiful day full of love and healing. After the ceremony, Mum treated me to a trip to the hairdressers and as I walked into the salon, the owner commented that I was positively glowing. And I could feel it too.

11

Too Young and Too Dumb

The summer of my A-Levels, after an argument with my dad's girlfriend over money, my dad kicked me out. It was déjà vu. Once again, here I was going through a significant transition in my life, only to find myself homeless.

I had always dreamed of going away to university. But months earlier when I presented the idea to Dad, he immediately shut the idea down and said it would be too expensive to live-in, and that he didn't approve of me living on campus. Disappointed, I accepted his ruling and changed my selection, applying instead to the most local institution I could find, where I would be able to commute from home every day. But now that I was no longer living in the catchment area, I was set to lose my university place.

A few weeks prior, I had learnt that I had secured a placement offer at my first uni option, on account of my grades (B, B, C). I wondered if my grades were some kind of serendipitous sign that one day that would be the acronym of my place of work. I wanted to have faith and believe it one day could be a possibility, but my vision was blighted by my current state of affairs.

My smarts and education were supposed to carry me through to my long-anticipated purpose and secure my life-affirming destiny, and yet I felt as though no matter how hard I tried, the critical stages of my master plan were constantly under threat and at risk of failing catastrophically.

With my car packed full of all my worldly possessions, with no idea of my next move, distraught, I left Dad's house and called Mum. As I sobbed hysterically down the phone, she assured me that we would figure things out together and that until we did, I could stay at her house. Relieved and emotionally spent, I thanked her and agreed to make my way over there. Before hanging up, she told me she loved me and ended the call by saying earnestly, "Don't worry, Nic, no matter what, we are going to make sure you go to uni!"

And true to her word, we made it happen. For the next few weeks, Mum helped me complete and submit a last-minute application for Kingston University—my original first choice, before Dad had instructed me to look more locally, thus pushing it down to second place on my selection list.

It took weeks and several phone calls and letters to the other university to explain my complicated situation and request to be released from their admissions list. I don't think requesting to have a conditional offer revoked was a common occurrence and I think the university administrator was quite miffed by my unusual request, before eventually honouring it.

In the meantime, Mum helped me apply for student loans and open a student bank account, she helped me select my halls of residence and research the university and potential courses online. Now completely estranged from Dad and only surviving on a part-time wage, Mum's circle of friends did a whip round and prepared an extensive going away care package, complete with pots and pans, utensils, toiletries and bedroom essentials. I was so grateful. Everything had happened so fast that it almost felt surreal by the time my induction paperwork arrived and Mum and I found ourselves at Orientation Day.

Mum and I kept pinching each other with excitement as we followed the tour around campus. I got to see where I would be living; luxury ensuite accommodation, communal kitchen, and allocated parking, a stone's throw from the River Thames, in a picturesque, beautiful part of town. We were then escorted around the main campus where I would be taking classes in English Language and Drama studies.

They had an impressive Arts & Humanities program, the buildings were modern and spacious, and the technology in the library and media facilities was state of the art. The university ran a free shuttle bus service to ferry students back and forth in-between periods from campus to the halls of residence, which eliminated any issues with parking, which was both expensive and scarce. It was ideal and finally felt like everything was coming together.

On moving in day, Mum and I packed up each of our cars, filled to the brim with all my newly purchased and gifted essentials to start my new life, and set off on our 90-minute car journey towards the South of the river. I was beaming the widest smile known to man when we pulled up in tandem outside my new digs—my new home for the next nine months.

The sun was shining, and I was undeniably buzzing as we began offloading the two cars of all my things and transporting them up to my room on the first floor. Every time I returned to my room, I let out an involuntary sigh of relief; it was happening, I was getting my happily ever after.

Most first-time home leavers on that day would probably have experienced some nerves and anxiety surrounding leaving home for the first time, but I'd had a two-year head start, and with no viable alternative, I was all in! This wasn't just a new address; this move was a lifeline, and so I grabbed hold of it with both hands and wasn't about to let go.

Chris caught the train down to meet us and on arrival joined the unloading operation. I eye-flirted with new flatmates and potential new friends as we met in the communal kitchen and stairwells, holding doors open for one another, our parents greeting one another with brief pleasantries and introductions as they beamed with pride. It was like the first day of school and Mum and Chris seemed just as excited as I was.

For the first time, I had to make weird decisions like which cupboard I wanted for my crockery and which I wanted for my sundries. I had to think about where to place the waste bin in my room and if my figurines and books suited their allocated placements on the shelf. They were small decisions, but to me, it was a coming of age. It was up to me, no longer bound by the decisions of the homeowner or an overbearing parent, this was all me, it was mine and I loved every square foot of my tiny, temporary oasis.

As I returned to the car to unload another box, I saw the excitement fade from Mum's face as she terminated a phone call on her mobile. Moments after she told me that Granny had had another fall and was in the hospital. Looking back now, I feel immense guilt that at the time I wasn't more concerned. She had fallen before but she had always recovered, she was a survivor, and so I didn't panic. As Mum left for the hospital with Chris, I returned to my room to finish unpacking and settle into my new home, waving them off from the window.

This may have been the first time that I was truly excited to be on my own. It soon became evident that all the freshers on campus felt the same way about their newfound freedom and for several days before the term officially started it felt like an unsupervised, never-ending party zone. For me though, I was just happy to celebrate feeling safe, and secure and having my life back on track.

In the coming weeks, I began settling into uni life, finding my way around campus and familiarising myself with the lecturers and the complex online homework portal. Outside of class, I got to know my flatmates and neighbours and made friends with a friendly bunch of girls from a few blocks down and enjoyed frequent nights out at the uni bar in the centre of town. I was adjusting well and landed a job at the local bowling alley as an 'alley cat', providing lane service and working on the bar.

The hours were long, sometimes not finishing until after midnight, and then having to be up for a 9 am lecture the next day was tough. Especially when I compared it to the fact that most of my friends didn't have to work at all. One of my flatmates told me that she had taken her student loan and put it in a high-interest savings account, with no intention of touching it for three years except to pay it back and cash in on her hefty interest payout. I and most of my friends were worlds apart, but that was something I was used to. Whether it was their family dynamics, lived experiences or finances, I always tended to be different. But that didn't faze me, I enjoyed working and the independence and financial security that came from it. I knew only too well that things could change in an instant and so I endeavoured to always keep my educational and employment commitments running in tandem to ensure maximum security.

Plus, the role at the bowling alley was fun, I enjoyed learning how to pull pints, fix lane errors and host kids' parties on Saturdays, honing my artistic skills of face painting and balloon modelling. Besides, the place was lively, and the customer tips were generous. I loved being able to immerse myself completely in my new life and saw little reason to revisit London, unlike most of my mates, who ventured home for weekend stints to see family and childhood friends.

Mum and I spoke a few times a week. I'd tell her about my newly formed friendships and classes I was enjoying, and she would update me on London life and how Granny was doing. I was surprised when she said that after almost a month, she still hadn't been discharged; her recovery didn't usually take this long, I thought.

Then one day out of the blue, Mum called and told me that all the family were being advised to come to the hospital. She said that she had put off telling me that Granny's condition was worsening so that I could focus on my studies. So, I knew that for her to be calling it had to be serious, and so I made the trip back to London and headed straight to the hospital.

It felt weird to be back in London. I had been enjoying my new life in my bubble for weeks and hadn't really given my old life much thought, so it seemed strange to suddenly be back in familiar surroundings. But living in my bubble had its disadvantages. I had become naive as to what was going on, and it wasn't until I was standing alone in the hospital room at the foot of Granny's bed, that

I suddenly realised the gravity of the situation. I took a sharp intake of breath and had to remind myself to breathe.

She looked so weak, and frail compared to her usual chatty and upbeat self. As tears welled up in my eyes, the reality hit me that this would be the last time I would be with her, here, like this. I told her I loved her, trying to disguise the quiver in my voice, unsure if she could hear me, but praying that she could. I bent down and kissed her before turning and running out of the room.

I couldn't possibly contemplate saying the actual words goodbye, not now, not ever. I felt like the bones in my body were breaking into a thousand pieces as I grew weaker and more faint by the second. I fled down the back staircase and down past the service elevator to avoid bumping into any relatives that were intending to visit at the same time.

Frantic, I got lost in the maze of staff-only corridors and emergency exits, as I darted about erratically, trying to escape—the building becoming a metaphor for my state of mind.

Gasping for air, I emerged onto the street, unsure of where I was. I walked and walked for miles until I finally found my car. I got in shaking and inconsolable and drove in the direction of the motorway heading straight back to uni. London had nothing for me anymore.

A few days before she died, Granny had given Mum a card to give to me. In it, she told me how proud she was of me in all my achievements and most recently starting university. To this day, I still can't read it without crying because I can tell from her handwriting, her health was failing. Her beautiful cursive, now faint and slanting down the page. And it will forever ache my heart to think that even on her deathbed, she was thinking of me. It was inconceivable for me to contemplate how I would go on without her.

In the weeks that followed, I withdrew from friends; I fell behind on assignments; I stopped answering my phone and participating in class. I didn't want to see or talk to anyone, I couldn't. I walked around campus with an intentionally unapproachable expression, deterring classmates and lecturers from engaging with me. The pain felt unbearable, and my promising new life was slipping away from me; the only difference this time was, that I genuinely didn't care. And then, for the third time in my life, my hair began to fall out.

The next few months, things were touch and go and just before the end of the first year of uni, I had managed to regain some focus and friends and pull my grades up just enough to qualify for second year enrolment, with the caveat that I passed my resits in the summer.

Life began to slowly improve. I made friends with a large social group of guys and girls from the 'ghetto-fabulous' campus five minutes away. The site was no frills and basic and the rent was considerably less than mine, there were no ensuites here! But the atmosphere had a buzz and there was a real comradery amongst everyone that lived there. Despite initially being snubbed as the boujee girl from down the block, I was soon given an honorary pass and accepted into the group, and for the first time since moving to uni, I felt like I had really found my clique.

With no contact from Dad and communication with Mum off and on and then off again, I immersed myself in my studies and spent more and more time with my new friends. I had started attending a new church in South London with one of my classmates. It was a vibrant Pentecostal church with a congregation of close to 1,000 with four services on a Sunday. The youth pastors were young and engaging and there was something about it that felt like home. Maybe it was the smell of Jamaican patties wafting in from the foyer or maybe it was the familial patois spoken by the elders as they busied around the large building. But whatever it was, it was another reason I didn't have to venture back home and another step in the direction of my new life.

Soon after I broke up with my boyfriend from back home (long distance after eight months had taken its toll) I started dating a popular guy on campus. Our friends dubbed us 'Posh and Becks' and I was surprised by how many people commented on how good we looked together—not something I had ever considered as a requirement!

Becks and I would see each other every day and hang out with the same big group of friends. It was easy and our friendship blossomed alongside our relationship as I told him about my faith, and we shared life experiences and compared our family dynamics and dysfunctions. We understood and appreciated one another.

He told me that he was attracted to my street smarts and independence which excelled me beyond my years. He said he admired my strength and resilience and applauded me for all I had achieved so far despite all of life's setbacks. In turn, I appreciated his wholesome nature. He possessed an innocence and trustworthiness that was endearing. Not shy, but not an extrovert either, he was the perfect balance of confidence and humility. Much like the theory of yin and yang, (and like my parents) we were attracted to one another's opposing qualities.

Becks was family-orientated and dependable and had a simplistic, laid-back approach to people and life. We were so different but seemed to share the same goal and that was to love and be loved.

When year one drew to a close and everyone returned home before the start of the new semester, I was faced with the reality that once again I had nowhere to go. Then out of the blue, Becks called and said he had been talking things over with his mum and that she had agreed to let me stay with them for the summer. I was relieved and a little dubious. I had never lived with a guy before, let alone their mother too. But I had no other viable options and at least they wanted me I thought.

Becks still had a few weeks left on his university tenancy, so in the beginning, it was just his mum and me, pottering around in their double-fronted detached house in North West London. She went out of her way to make me feel welcome and told me she loved having female company in a household where she had only raised boys. We never ran out of things to talk about and would sit for hours in her extravagant bedroom with bath ensuite, talking about everything and nothing.

Whilst helping her clear out her wardrobe, she would intermittently pause to showcase her impressive fashion collection and would randomly unearth forgotten finds with elaborate back stories and often gift me personal trinkets and coupons that she discovered as she went.

Becks would come home on the weekends, and I would assimilate into wifey mode. I would drive him around on errands and do laundry. In the evenings, we would watch movies on the big screen in the lounge and go for midnight walks or late-night drives for take-aways. We pooled our money like a married couple and booked weekends away and bought each other elaborate gifts to show our affections.

But being in London, things between us weren't the same, it came with so many distractions for Becks. He was always out, catching up with friends and checking up on family he had missed since leaving town. We increasingly spent less and less time together and I began to feel more like a nagging wife than a new love interest.

The honeymoon bubble had started to dissolve. He frequently accepted invitations to BBQ's and christenings and attended social engagements without me. Back at uni, we had always done things together and moved around in the same social group; going out on co-ed nights out and attending drink-ups as a couple. But in London, things were different, and it felt like we were slowly drifting apart. His world was getting bigger and mine was getting smaller.

Oblivious, he would report back to me about the events of the night before, casually relaying the propositions of female friends and mates that attempted to lead him astray, detailing his jovial, lacklustre protests, that would only serve to infuriate me and give rise to my simmering insecurities. He would tell me about his friends and their criticisms of me and our relationship and unwittingly recap their expressed desire to liberate him back into the world of singledom so that they could enjoy an unrestricted 'hot boy summer'.

His cavalier approach to his friends' lack of respect for our relationship and his reluctance to define boundaries and defend me left me unimpressed at best and in an emotional downward spiral at my very worst.

I thought Becks was too much of a people-pleaser, naive and forgiving, meanwhile, he felt I was too outspoken, begrudging and cynical. Opposites were no longer attracting. We constantly argued and every time he threatened to break up with me or stormed out, I relived unresolved feelings of abandonment and rejection from my childhood. Becks was my world, my lifeline, my family and my home. Without him, I had nothing.

As a result of my insecurities, I became even more dependent on him as he increasingly pulled away, which only fuelled my self-doubt and catapulted us into a vicious cycle. It wasn't long before we began to realise that looking good together was no indication that we were meant to be.

Whilst continuous in-fighting ensued, I battled to also maintain the perfect outward appearance of a happy, healthy relationship, paranoid that any chink in our armour would be used against me and exploited by the baying crowd that did not want to see us stay together, which now even included his mum. Preoccupied with keeping up appearances, determined to prove all of my haters and his overzealous admirers wrong, I failed to see the signs that the relationship had turned toxic and that I was no longer OK.

After intermittent break-ups, I was left feeling like there was nothing worth living for and I often felt like Becks was only staying with me or willing to reconcile to prevent me from doing the unthinkable. He felt trapped and I felt worse knowing that he was only staying with me to keep me alive. Frustrated by the situation, Becks' temper worsened as his patience waned and he would often lash out verbally or punch walls and break things. He was like a caged animal, desperate to escape, conflicted by the potential outcome.

Devastated by the monster I seemed to be creating, I would give him his out and tell him to leave, but just as I had begun to process moving on, days later, he would turn up at my part-time job or at the flat I moved into with friends, with bouquets of flowers and cards declaring his unfailing love. And other times, I would intercept him at the end of his work shift or after his evening class, pleading for another chance. We had become bound by co-dependency, trapped in a cycle neither of us knew how to break.

We wanted to be together, but we knew we brought out the worst in each other. Too immature and ill-equipped, we were overwhelmed by the adult weight of the relationship and all the baggage we brought to it. We knew being together was hard but the only thing that felt harder was the gut-wrenching thought of breaking up.

There were countless nights that we would stay up talking, contemplating our fate, deliberating until the early hours of the morning, regularly missing out on critical sleep for an important exam the next day or valuable preparation time for a project. We were two broken people, trying to make one another whole.

As if my relationship issues weren't bad enough, my final year of studies managed to zap any energy I had left in reserve. I had always liked acting, and I got the impression over the years from performing arts school to high school right through to university that I was a pretty talented performer.

But I always dreaded the group project dynamic; having to brainstorm and creatively collaborate with others, forcing me to skilfully de-escalate power struggles and navigate the right balance of contribution without control—my grade hanging in the balance and dependant on the cooperation and participation of others was beyond daunting as a prospect.

The final end-of-year group production was gruelling and at times felt soul-destroying. Working in a group with five other opinionated, blunt and creatively passionate women pushed me to the brink of exhaustion. I dreaded the tense atmosphere of rehearsals, and by the time performance day arrived, I was barely speaking to the rest of the cast.

Insistent on challenging myself by being the only one willing to play the role of a man, I went against the approval of the rest of the group, immediately putting me at odds with the collective. I decided to write my character a monologue scene, when it became apparent that I would not feature in much of the remainder of the script and had little cooperation from my cast to interact with the male character I had created.

My character was Joe, a fictional 21-year-old soldier set during the First World War. My scene consisted of me talking to a chair laid flat on the floor that I used to symbolise the body of my dead brother that I had discovered on the battlefield. For nine whole minutes, I was able to capture the audience's attention and suspend their disbelief whilst speaking to a horizontal, inanimate object.

In the final moments when my character started to cry, you could hear a pin drop in the auditorium. I knew my audience was captivated as the lights dimmed and went to blackout, followed by an almighty deafening roar from the audience.

After the performance, friends came over from the audience and congratulated me on a stellar performance, several of them commented on their fascination that I was able to cry on cue and asked me how I was able to do it. I didn't know what to say. I had never really unpacked the process of method acting before and didn't know how to break it down. I never had to think of something sad to cry about, instead, I drew on the all-too-familiar feeling of sadness to evoke the emotion.

In a row later that night, Becks told me he was unmoved by my performance because he had seen my tears once too often.

A few weeks later, one of my drama tutors called and told me that I and only one other person in the entire year of around 50 students, had been selected by an acting scout for a summer scholarship to the Student Drama Festival, in North Yorkshire. She said the scout was extremely impressed by my performance and looked forward to meeting me at summer camp.

I was shocked and couldn't believe that I had been selected. With a generous advance loan from my drama teacher, which I vowed to pay back (and did), that summer, I went to Scarborough and attended masterclasses with Timothy West, Sam West and Prunella Scales. I felt honoured to be in the presence of such talent and privileged to be given the opportunity to perfect my craft. The festival signalled the end of the year and the end of uni—what a climactic ending. I was going out on a high, despite a tumultuous three years!

Becks had another year to complete his four-year course, so, I moved out of my place I was sharing with two friends in Kingston and returned to London without him. Renting a room in a shared house, I began to reflect on what I wanted for my future and how I was going to set the wheels in motion to go after it. I knew if I was going to get the future I wanted, there were some things I was going to have to leave in the past. And so, after two and a half years together, I decided to end things between Becks and I for good.

Now away from our concentrated uni environment and our toxic bubble, I finally felt strong enough to walk away. When it travelled through the grapevine to our friends and foes that we had broken up, I think everyone was surprised to hear that I had actually ended the relationship and not the other way around. I had come to accept that we both needed out of what had become an unhealthy relationship. We both needed to walk away to secure our own happiness and maintain our sanity and that meant breaking the cycle.

But to let go, I was going to have to break all ties. So, I did. I lost contact with his family and most of our mutual friends. If this was going to work, I needed to make a clean break.

University had taken its toll; I had experienced grief, loss, stress and heartbreak and for me to have half a chance of a fresh start, I had to re-focus on myself and get back on track with the master plan. I told myself I was at the final hurdle now; school, college and uni were complete, and now it was time for the final piece of the puzzle—the career of my dreams.

I graduated in October of that year, ten marks away from a first-class degree. Under normal circumstances, the over-achiever in me would have been gutted but at this point, I was just grateful to have made it through, against all odds and there had been a lot of odds!

In the private dressing room for graduates, I was dressed by an assistant in my cap and gown. As she left, I turned to face the mirror and the reflection of a happy, confident accomplished woman smiled back at me. The re-invention felt complete. I sobbed like a baby for two whole minutes, before attempting to compose myself and salvage my non-waterproof mascara and winged liquid eyeliner.

At that moment, I thought about that little girl with skinny legs, frizzy blondie-brown hair with big lips who was bullied and began to hate herself. I thought about the teenager that spent years reinventing herself trying to find acceptance and love, often feeling as though she wasn't liked and didn't fit in. I reminisced about all the times I felt like I couldn't go on and felt like checking out altogether.

The woman standing now in front of the mirror didn't reflect any of those things and yet this pivotal moment was all the more significant because it represented them all in a vacuum of time. As I steadied myself to leave the dressing room, I thought about all the people who couldn't be there with me, who would have been so proud of where I was standing or that I was still standing at all.

I emerged from the dressing room to reunite with Mum, Camille and Chris in the foyer of the Grand Hall of the Barbican, where they were patiently standing alongside other excited, expectant relatives waiting for a first glimpse of their adorned graduand.

As soon as Mum laid eyes on me, she rushed towards me, we embraced and immediately began crying happy tears as she gushed and told me over and over how proud she was of me. Moments later, I walked across the stage and received my degree. In awe, I sat back down in my seat, almost too overcome to read my coveted scroll as I held it in my hands. This didn't just feel like an academic accreditation, this was the ticket to my new life in the palm of my hands. This piece of paper represented hope for my future.

It wasn't just about having a degree or being able to brag about my studious aptitude, this was a triumph and a blessing from God; it was the start of my journey to my new life. I was turning the page to a whole new chapter and not looking back. This piece of paper symbolised my Exodus.

12

Adulting

I was a graduate now—a big girl in an even bigger wide world. It was day one of the rest of my life and after reaching the dizzy heights of academic success, I had suddenly been thrust into the uncharted territories of adulthood and was starting at ground zero.

The bonus was (as always) I had a plan. I had a laser-focused ambition to pool all my efforts into pursuing and achieving my dream of becoming a TV presenter—this had long been my ambition, after abandoning plans to be an illustrator and author of children's books sometime around high school. I don't know when exactly I settled on the idea of this career vocation, but I couldn't think of anything else that would even come close to topping it.

I studied the craft as I watched with admiration and learnt how my favourite hosts on Saturday morning TV spoke with ease, presenting entertaining and engaging links in between segments on the latest popular culture music channels. I was inspired, I had found my niche. It was official—mission 'Become a TV presenter' was in full effect.

When I announced my decided career plan to friends and family, they were surprised. A stage performer all these years, many had assumed I would naturally continue in the same vein, destined for a career 'treading the boards'. I loved acting but had spent so many years fixated on reinventing myself in attempts to win people's adoration, I was done with the concept of playing a role and the thought of being able to simply be myself and get paid for it was liberating.

I had watched enough documentaries and celebrity biopics to know that the road to fame and fortune was never a straightforward one and often began with humble beginnings, so I took a realist's approach and accepted that if I was going to achieve ultimate TV stardom, it wouldn't happen overnight. So, first things first, I needed to pay the rent, which is why straight out of uni, I took the first job

I could get. I was hired as a department supervisor at the iconic Top Shop fashion store in the heart of London.

It paid well but the demands of working full-time for the first time were a challenge. I was assigned to manage a team of 15, many of whom were more senior in age and several of whom took exception to my new appointment. Having worked occasionally at the store as a casual sales temp previously, now returning with a role in management changed the dynamic completely with my once friendly co-workers.

I was often excluded from department socials and became the topic of shop-floor gossip because now I was the boss, which meant I was on the other side of friendly lines. I powered through, despite often feeling out of my depth, struggling to adjust to management life and the long gruelling hours. Feeling overwhelmed and exhausted, I began suffering frequent migraines and more severe panic attacks and resorted to regularly hiding out in the staff toilets or taking extended breaks just to escape the dazzling showroom lights and overrun shop floor.

After a few months, I became so exhausted at even the thought of getting out of bed that I began to call in sick to work. A short while after that, I returned only to hand in my resignation. I was physically and emotionally exhausted. The next month when I couldn't come up with the rent, my landlord terminated my lease and once again, I was homeless.

A loving family and a sense of security and belonging was something that I had craved all my life and I felt like a failure that somehow, I had never been able to find or create it.

Mum and I weren't speaking again, and I hadn't had communication with Dad in over three years. I was clueless as to what I was going to do, so I got in my car and drove and drove and drove. I had no idea where I was going or what I was going to do when I got there. I drove until my petrol tank was almost completely empty and pulled over for the night in a motorway service station. I found a secluded, dimly lit area, away from the lorries and the amenities and switched off the engine. Climbing into the backseat, freezing cold and starving, I lay down and sobbed.

I was a failure. I had attempted the first rung on my ladder of success and had not even gotten off the ground. I couldn't believe it was all unravelling and that once again, I was at rock bottom.

With no other viable prospects, the next day, I returned to the council. The assessment officer asked if I had children and I told her I didn't and that I had just graduated from university. Unimpressed, she sighed and said, "That's a shame you don't have kids, that would've been much better."

Disappointed, she continued to thumb through my paperwork, pausing infrequently to scribble down notes or pencil in a cross where appropriate. Demoralised and distraught, I watched and waited as my future was determined by box ticks and checklists.

I was allocated a room in a shared house where I would live with the landlord and his family and another tenant in a modest three-bedroom house in Greenford. I sold my car to generate some savings, another humbling slight to my independence. The family were pleasant, and the home was comfortable and yet I was extremely uncomfortable. Sharing a kitchen with my landlord and his family felt strange. I always felt like I was in the way or trying to make myself invisible. Sneaking in and out of the bathroom during brief intervals, storing my crockery in my room until everyone had gone to bed and trying to watch the TV on subtitles late at night so as not to disturb anyone. After living alone for so long it should have felt good to be living with a family, but it didn't. It wasn't home. I didn't belong and the only reason they were tolerating me was because they were being paid to.

Soon after Mum and I were back on speaking terms and she helped me move out and secure a deposit for a quaint studio flat, just a road away from Grandad's old shop. It felt symbolic that in some way I had come full circle, back to where it had all started. The area was a little dicier than I remembered, the flat was tiny, and the neighbours were noisy, but it was home.

I immediately joined a slew of recruitment agencies and frequently scoured the classifieds looking for jobs. I had a month before the second month's rent was due and I wasn't going to 'mess up' again. I went to the job centre on the high road on a daily basis, printing off job ads on their electronic self-serve ticket machine, before heading to the local internet café, armed with my CV on a USB stick and applied to jobs for hours on end.

Within a couple of weeks, I got an interview at an upscale hair and beauty salon in Fulham. After an unorthodox interview, which included an unexpected and very undignified head massage demo, I was informed I had got the job. As I left I internally cringed as I caught sight of my hair in utter disarray in one of their ten-foot grand mirrors by the entrance. But was pleasantly distracted when the manager, escorting me to the door asked when I could start and I didn't hesitate in replying, "Right away!"

My new place of employment was a swanky, luxury salon complete with spa and boujee clientele to match. It was definitely an insight into how the other half lived. I couldn't have dreamed of ever being able to experience any of the treatments on the price list had it not been for my 'free staff discount'.

The salon was run by a highly-strung, flamboyant, American hair stylist turned business owner (we'll call her Angie), and the salon was managed by an also American, unconventional manager, we'll call her Megan.

Angie was particular about everything, and my OCD didn't even come close to her idealistic standards and perfectionism. She was meticulous about everything, from how the towels on the shelves were folded to how we positioned a customer's refreshments on their tray. The scrutiny and criticism was relentless. Angie was the first and last person to ever tell me I wasn't warm or bubbly enough!

She would critique my friendliness with customers and nit-pick constantly. She would resort to cold-calling the salon just to check up on me and frequently score my telephone manner and response time. In my appraisal with her and Megan, Angie told me she thought my hair always looked dirty and greasy. I was stunned at the blatant and unprofessional macro-aggression, not to mention being further offended when I found out later that Megan had shared this information with the entire staff team. Despite Angie claiming to be a world-renowned hair stylist, if she had taken the time to learn anything at all about chemically relaxed afro hair, she would have known that shiny, oiled hair was an indication of good health and nourished cuticles. Had it been dirty, it would have been the opposite, dry and dull.

Shocked and embarrassed, I sheepishly informed her I had washed my hair the night before and it was certainly not dirty or greasy.

As well as being a receptionist, Angie and Megan, treated me like the general dog's body. I was expected to do it all: fix every technical problem, take the week's takings on foot to the bank, purchase a brand new 12kg hi-fi system complete with speakers and carry it two miles down the high street back to the salon when our regular stereo malfunctioned during Saturday service, as well as regularly filling in for the juniors, washing clients' hair and performing their signature Indian head massages whilst fielding telephone calls. It was relentless.

But the event that overshadowed all others was the morning of the re-launch. I arrived early only to find the salon furniture still covered in dust sheets and only half of the intended painted walls complete. As I entered the salon, I found Megan in the middle of a spirited argument with the contracted painter, who had just told her that he certainly wouldn't be finished by opening time (in 30 minutes) and probably not even be complete by the launch that evening.

As I looked around the salon in disbelief at the many bare and unpainted walls, the argument intensified at the front of the shop, and then in an instant, the painter picked up his things and walked out, slamming the door behind him. Megan, hot on his heels, followed, stopping in the doorway to continue the exchange of insults followed by her threats to discredit his business and sue him.

She was too enraged in that moment for me to attempt to tell her that no one threatens to 'sue' anyone here in the UK and that unlike in her hometown of Texas, that word didn't carry the same weight in Fulham.

Everything about that day was chaotic. Megan frantically instructed me to call all the customers and cancel their appointments for the day and then to my amazement, she told me afterwards to call all the stylists and tell them not to come in but to assure them they would be compensated a day's pay. In between turning away walk-in customers and answering the phone, I was ordered up the ladder to complete the painting myself.

I think it was at that moment at the top of the ladder, with my brand new sneakers covered in paint, fraught and dizzy from paint fumes that I decided that enough was enough and that I would imminently be handing in my notice. At around lunchtime, one of the stylists popped in to see how we were getting on with the one-man refurb. She kindly brought me my favourite can of pop to cheer me up and went on to inform Megan and me that she and the other stylists were all hanging out in the summer garden of the pub across the road.

That's it, I'm done! I thought. But this time, I would plan my exit plan so that I had something to move on to. I thought of it as jumping lily pads and endeavoured to always secure the next jump before I made my move, so as not to end up in the same predicament as before. Right mission 'Get the heck out of here' had been activated.

A few months later, when I had been at the salon for around a year, I landed a receptionist job in an elite PR fashion house in affluent Kensington. I hadn't lost sight of my overarching goal to become a TV presenter, but in the meantime, this move made sense; the salary was much better, the company had great benefits and future prospects, not to mention we got to pour over exclusive fashion samples all day and rub shoulders with some of the biggest industry leaders in the business. Plus, no more Angie and no more Megan, what more convincing did I need!

Whilst working at the PR company, I worked flat-out in my spare time to do what people say is a necessity in showbiz and 'Get my face out there!'. I joined every affordable talent database available, signed up for subscriptions like *The Stage* newspaper and tirelessly applied to talent agencies. When I wasn't working, I was auditioning and applying to talent postings as if it were my full-time job.

I saved £20 of my weekly wage so that I could take street dance classes at a dance studio in Covent Garden once a week. Taking dance classes allowed me to rekindle my passion for my first love—performing. In addition to that, the studio had a talent jobs board on the top floor. There they listed a whole array of upcoming castings and audition links, which I perused on a weekly basis along with all the other budding performers who gently pushed and nudged one another out of the way to get access to the board and scribble down casting call details.

There was a hint of cliqueness at the studio. An all too familiar feeling that instantly reminded me of my many experiences at various stage schools growing up. I didn't fit in; I didn't have the branded leotards and matching leggings or know any of the instructors by name. The professional dancers kissed and greeted one another as they cut in line to be closer to the mirror and shared tales of their latest performance accomplishments. I was out of place—a budding TV presenter, taking street dance classes in my spare time whilst working as a receptionist at a PR company, so I kept myself to myself.

Sometimes the studio would hold auditions on site and the long line of prospective stars lining the halls would draw my attention and lead me to investigate further to find out what all the commotion was in aid of.

After a typically gruelling street dance class one afternoon, red-faced and sweaty, I made my way to the changing rooms. En route, I noticed a mass of dancers congregating outside a classroom door. I walked up to the door to read the sign posted outside and discovered an audition for a lead female dancer for a music advert was underway. I paused and contemplated what to do. Fighting all of my insecurities, I joined the lengthy queue.

Every waiting moment, as I stepped closer and closer to the audition room door, I became more and more anxious. Internally battling with thoughts brought on by the all-too-familiar imposter syndrome.

What are you doing, Nicola, you are not classically or professionally trained, how can you compete against these girls, why would they pick you?

I fought to keep my internal voice of self-doubt at bay and appear upbeat and confident every time the creative director appeared in the doorway and called the next girl in.

Every time he would return to the room accompanied by the next auditionee, I would let out a sigh of relief and repeat the cycle of flip-flopping back and forth in my head, trying to decide if I should hold my nerve or abandon the line before he returned and spare myself the inevitable humiliation. And then before I knew it, it was too late, I was next.

As the door swung open, my heart began racing as I braced myself for the calling of my name. He looked down at his clipboard and just at the moment he looked up, he was distracted by a familiar face in the line calling his name and instantaneously beckoned them forward. Hugging and chit-chatting, they stood in the doorway before walking arm-in-arm into the audition room. Just as he was about to close the door, it was as if something dawned on him, and as an afterthought, he looked back at me and said nonchalantly, "Sorry hun, you'll be next!"

And without missing a beat, I smiled sweetly and replied, "Don't worry, I'll be worth the wait!"

As quick as the words had left my mouth, I was shocked by the seemingly confident declaration I had just made. Equally stunned, the creative director stopped dead in his tracks in the doorway and looked back at me. I froze. *Had I just blown my chance?*

He stared at me for a few seconds whilst I held my nerve and maintained eye contact whilst awaiting my fate, and without responding he closed the door.

After what felt like an eternity, he reappeared in the doorway, with no clipboard in sight, embraced his friend-auditionee and immediately locked eyes with me and exclaimed, "Right, missy, you're up!"

As I followed him into the dance studio, he re-joined the other judges behind a makeshift desk and directed me to introduce myself to the camera that was being operated on a tripod in the corner. He then announced to the room, "Apparently, this one is worth waiting for!" His subtle smirk made it impossible for me to deduce whether he was impressed by my boldness or was in fact mocking me.

"Come on Nic!" I told myself. "You can't mess this up now, not with that introduction!"

The anticipation in the room was palpable as the judges studied me up and down and I waited for the music to start. And just before I could overthink the situation any further, the music started and instantly, I was in the zone! Showcasing my best freestyle moves, playing up to the camera, exuding confidence and executing every unrehearsed move with definition and flair, I danced my heart out for the next 60 seconds like my life depended on it.

As the creative director thanked me and explained the selection process and I left the room, his poker face gave nothing away. I walked back to the changing room (an hour later than planned) and felt content, I had given it my all and for that I was proud.

Later that night, I got a call, it was the creative director. Over the phone, he seemed different, warmer, more enthused. A stark contrast from his earlier reserved demeanour. He congratulated me on an impressive audition and told me that I had got the job as lead dancer in a compilation music advert and would be travelling to Manchester to shoot the commercial. The director's fan favourite was cast to be my backing dancer.

Two weeks later, I boarded the coach full of cast and crew as we left our pick-up point in London and were driven to the filming location. I got my first taste of stardom when we disembarked the vehicle several hours later in the late hours of the evening outside an exclusive nightclub in the city centre and were escorted to set, like VIPs in front of queuing patrons. We were greeted and taken backstage by the venue manager, and I entered a room where the word 'talent' was scribbled on an A4 piece of paper on the door. I hadn't reached the dizzy heights of showbiz yet, but I resolved, it was a promising start!

Inside the makeshift dressing room, I was introduced to 'my team' which consisted of a stylist for wardrobe and another for hair and make-up. I was invited into the make-up chair and primped and preened. It felt surreal as people ran around me, members of the crew who seemed to know my name momentarily stopping by to give me stage directions as well as the shoot editor to brief me on the script and to double check I was happy with everything. *Was I happy with everything? I was ecstatic!*

When the advert aired and I saw myself on television, it was like nothing I had felt before. I felt like my dreams were finally being realised and it was even more encouraging that others seemed to have recognised my potential too. The achievement was the ultimate validation I needed that all the hard work had been worth it, and I finally had something tangible to show for my pie-in-the-sky dreams.

I recorded the advert on a DVD and played it for enthusiastic family members and friends whenever they visited, as they cooed, "Rewind it!" and "Play it again!"

I hadn't spoken to Dad in what seemed like forever at this point, but I would hear through the grapevine later, that he would proudly share with family and friends my latest TV exploits. It was nice to know he was supporting my dreams albeit from a distance.

Whilst still working at the PR firm, I was cast as a presenter for a TV show on SKY, after a gruelling all-day audition process. I travelled to Euston Road after work to a small studio to film the weekly episodes. I presented the TV show for peanuts, learning scripts in my lunch break and on the train commute.

The money I was paid for the TV show wasn't enough to quit my day job, but I considered the exposure and the by-product of building my content a worthy trade off. I was creating a brand, increasing my network, and bringing together all those other critical elements they talk about in TED talks and the like, for budding talent.

Now with a well-paid job and a small-earning side hustle, for the first time, I was able to save some money and buy my own car and finally travel. Having missed out on so many family reunions abroad throughout the years, I was finally in a position to splurge, a little.

Mum, Sean, Camille and I planned a trip to Spain and were so excited to be going on our first family holiday in over ten years.

I loved everything about Spain: the weather, the language and the people. Uninspired by the traditional 18–30s English bars on the strip, I convinced Camille to come with me to visit the Spanish bars off the beaten track. We had an absolute blast every night and got to try out our 'Spanglish' with the locals and accommodating bar staff.

On the last night of the holiday, I met a local guy a few years older than me, in one of the native bars. He made a beeline for me by the crowded bar and proceeded to bat away all other male attention, telling them we were an item. I was instantly attracted to his confidence and the way he took charge, ordering us drinks as he paid me compliments and made me blush as he told his friends I was his future wife. His English was really good (although he didn't think so) and he graciously humoured me as I attempted to demonstrate my attempts at conversing in his native tongue.

He agreed to follow our taxi back to the hotel after I declined his offer for a ride, and after he bid Camille good night in the foyer of the hotel, we sat outside and talked until the sun began to come up. When I told him I was going to retire to bed, he insisted that we exchange numbers before giving me a kiss on the cheek and driving away.

The whole flight back to London, I daydreamed about my 'holiday romance' and smiled with excitement as we landed, and my phone pinged with a message from my Spanish Casanova.

In the coming weeks, Holiday Romance and I kept in touch, speaking over the phone and emailing one another. We got by with the help of language dictionaries and online translation apps. After weeks of talking and Faceting, our feelings for one another quickly intensified and when he asked if we could make our relationship official, I said yes. The month after that he flew me out to Spain to visit.

He took me all over his home city and introduced me to his friends and family. I could see how much the trip meant to him and how much thought and planning he had put into it. I was touched, albeit a little overwhelmed. Things were moving so fast, and I didn't want to get hurt again. I graciously went along with things, as he showed me off and paraded me in front of his nearest and dearest and I did my best to make a good impression, practising my very recently acquired Spanish vocabulary to a seemingly impressed audience.

As he watched me adoringly from across the table, I got butterflies as I felt completely cherished and dare I say it, in love.

Momentary bouts of panic would flood my head and course around my body as I contemplated that things were moving too fast. I would battle to suppress these thoughts as I told myself not to overthink things and to just go with the flow—a skill that does not come naturally, but I gave it my best shot—I tried not to obsess, and to just live in the moment.

Then one afternoon, as we were getting ready for another evening of festivities, in the middle of repacking my suitcase, he stopped me and presented me with a tiny blue jewellery box. He had bought me jewellery before—a chain, a pair of personalised gold earrings he had designed himself, so I had no real cause for alarm. As he opened the box, I was distracted by the note that fell out of it and landed on the floor. Bending down to retrieve it, as I got closer, the only words I could make out that were in English, halfway down on the paper were 'genuine diamond'.

As I picked it up and turned back towards him, I was stunned to find him standing in close proximity with the box now sprained open in my direction and inside peering back at me was a sliver, round-cut diamond ring. Before I could stop him, he had proposed.

I thought back to the first time he had told me he loved me and how he reacted when I hesitated, emotionally breaking down and spiralling out of control. A lengthy argument followed where he accused me of not being genuine in my feelings for him and at one point even accused me of having an affair. For the first time, he appeared insecure, perceiving my caution as rejection and I contemplated the consequences of a repeat of former events.

I wanted to protect his fragile feelings and not cause a fight, so I internalised my doubts and anxiety and muttered a hesitant, "Yes."

I wore the ring for two days whilst I was out there, but it just didn't feel right. I felt pressured, blindsided, and dare I say it, regretful. It's not that I didn't want to marry him, we just needed to know each other better first before we made a lifelong commitment. I didn't want to divorce like my parents. I wanted a marriage that was going to stand the test of time and there was still so much we hadn't figured out yet, namely where we were going to live, for one.

Holiday Romance had a less progressive ideology when it came to gender roles and was adamant that he wanted me to not work and to stay at home instead and raise our future children, whilst he intended on setting up his own business and ultimately providing for the family. To some women, this might have sounded like a dream, but to me, it couldn't have been more of the makings of a nightmare. I had dreams of my own and none of them involved me staying home, barefoot and pregnant.

I had career aspirations, and I wasn't going to realise them as a housewife in a small Spanish town. I was finally breaking through and could see my dreams finally coming to fruition, but his plan only seemed to derail that—I mean how do you say TV presenter extraordinaire in Spanish! If we were going to get married, our futures had to marry up first.

The day before I returned to England, I plucked up enough courage to tell him that I couldn't marry him—not yet anyway and gave him back the ring. I assured him I didn't want to break up but that I needed more time. He took it surprisingly well and we were able to salvage the final day of the trip and agreed to put all conversations of our engagement and the M-word on ice.

After I returned home, we picked up right where we left off and the following month, it was his turn to visit me in the UK. He met my mum and reunited with Camille when we visited a local bowling alley and grabbed a bite to eat. I was so excited to show him the sights and for two full days, we were typical tourists around London. I took him on a night out to my favourite bar with friends and we went to Notting Hill Carnival where he was in his element, blending in with the crowd, dancing and drinking in the Bank Holiday sun.

The trip was going well and there had been no mention of the 'diamond elephant in the room' until one day he was unpacking his suitcase and a familiar blue box fell out of the inside pocket. I felt an instant lump in my throat. Shocked, I picked it up and asked him why he had brought it. Upset and emotional, he began a rant about me still not wanting to marry him and before I knew it, we were in a fully-fledged row.

As our voices continued to raise and we hurled insults and accusatory remarks, I had a flashback of me and Becks and abruptly stopped, dead in my tracks. This was how it started, the toxic, unhealthy cycle. I knew better this time around. I wasn't going to make the same mistake twice and so right there and then I took a deep breath and ended it. Reluctantly, he agreed to change his flight and get an earlier return ticket.

My holiday romance was over and two hours later, we unceremoniously parted ways as he left in a taxi, airport-bound.

13

Evolution

Determined to leave the world of fashion PR behind and to work more closely in media, I applied for the role of PA at Virgin Media and UKTV's head office in the West End in their ad sales company. I knew it was not the fast-track route to a role in front of the camera that I was hoping for, but I was content in the moment that it got me a step closer at least to working for a TV company. Plus, it made more sense on my CV, and it got me away from front-of-house and behind the 'veiled curtain'.

Arriving for my interview, I was taken aback by the impressive architecture and scale of the building. A stunning five-storey listed building in the heart of central London. The interior was even more remarkable and aesthetically pleasing than the exterior: modern and exuding luxury and opulence, from the high ceilings, and on-trend exposed natural brickwork, to the vibrant bespoke furniture and neutral faux rugs which lined the reception area.

Abstract art lined the walls along with awards, alongside huge plasma screens that hung from every wall, blasting music from a range of pop radio stations. The atmosphere was electric and vibrant. I was in awe, taking it all in, and was caught off-guard when Jenny, the hiring manager, appeared in the doorway and called my name.

Jenny was really friendly and put me at ease during the formal interview, in the grand boardroom. We bonded over being foodies and our shared taste in music. My discovery that she had previously worked for MTV was a bonus and I tried to curb my enthusiasm as she talked about what a great time she'd had working there and about the close friendships she had established there, that still existed years later.

The mood of the interview slightly shifted, and I began to feel uneasy when she began to quiz me about my passions and career goals. I talked about my love for art and writing and street dance and kept all answers about future aspirations administration related. I contemplated telling her about my new TV presenting gig but thought better of it. I was worried that it would go against me and hinder my chances of getting the job, not to mention trigger concerns that I would be more interested in hitting up her old black book of former MTV contacts than being a PA.

So, I kept shtum. I needed this job; my dreams were by no means on hold, but a woman still needed to pay her bills! Jenny called me later that day to tell me I had got the job. I thanked her over and over, before hanging up and jumping ecstatically up and down on the spot.

Excited and keenly early on my first day, I walked in through the grandiose double doors and offered my name at the reception desk. Moments later, Jenny greeted me and escorted me to the fifth floor and through to the open-plan office. The company consisted of around 70 driven 20–30-somethings, with a small fraction of directors in their early 40s and 50s at the top of the food chain.

Shortly after arriving, I was taken on what I was told was a traditional introductory tour, which I soon learnt consisted of being escorted around the entire office floor and introduced to every individual member of staff at their desk. Running out of charming originality, halfway around the circuit, I resorted to repeating the same introductory patter and found myself instantly replacing each name and face with the next.

I was surprised to discover on my office tour that I was one of only two Black people in the entire department. However, despite an evident lack of diversity, I felt comfortable. My years of experience attending schools as a minority had put me in good training and I had now gotten to the point where I noticed it but was rarely fazed by being the only brown face around the boardroom table. Some may see that as a triumph. Looking back now, I think it's quite tragic that I was so used to the lack of diversity, that I no longer paid attention to it.

Soon after the intros were complete, I was catapulted into the intricate, high-octane world of ad sales support which consisted of endless meetings, presentations, and training. By the end of the week, I was frazzled and felt like I had been cramming for an exam, stuck on a continuum of information overload.

I was assigned to support three teams totalling around 30 agents. They were a driven, ambitious, hardworking bunch that were friendly, but competitive, fun-spirited, and brutally honest in equal measure. As I watched how colleagues openly confronted one another on the 'sales floor', aggressively challenged each other's ideas in brainstorming sessions and intensely negotiated deals in meetings, I was taken aback. I had never worked in such a fast-paced, intense environment, and I realised very quickly that this was not the place for the faint-hearted.

If I stood any chance of surviving, I was going to have to develop a much thicker skin and be able to give as good as I got and that meant no more putting myself down or underselling my achievements—that wasn't going to do me any favours in this dog-eat-dog arena.

I made friends quickly within the team and felt a real sisterhood amongst a big group of female colleagues. We shared magazines and watched reality shows online together at lunchtime, we took extended toilet breaks together where we would gossip and share make-up tips and exchange hair tidies, before important client meetings and Thursday nights out.

Everyone was given a nickname whether you liked it or not and most of them, especially the ones assigned to the guys had convoluted back stories, which often involved some embarrassing drunken exploit or unattractive physical attribute. I had learnt it was better to accept your given nickname than to protest, which would only highlight your aversion to it, guaranteeing that it would inevitably stick with you for the entire length of your employment. Mine was 'Morrison', not massively original, but inoffensive too!

I successfully navigated how to ride the waves of the locker room banter and assimilate. Unperturbed by the many boozy Friday lunches and after work bar crawls, I watched on from the sidelines, soft drink in hand. I didn't exactly fit in, but I felt accepted, and I reconciled that that was good enough.

Barbara was my eccentric, quirky line manager. She was equally creative as she was wacky. She wore elaborate over-the-top outfits and had a haphazard yet endearing way about her. Barbara mentioned several times how happy she was to finally have a 'girl' on the team, and at our weekly routines, we were regularly taken off-piste as she digressed from conversations about her diary or upcoming projects to reveal the contents of shopping bags buried under her desk, showing off her latest vintage purchases, whilst whispering the extortionate price tags from behind her hand as if it were classified information.

Other times, I enjoyed her recalling in detail her scandalous exploits of all night raves and wild parties from her heyday in the 80s! She was a great line manager, albeit with some slight tendencies of micro-management, which I quickly forgave, convinced it was more as a result of her chaotic work style than an indication of a real lack of trust.

In one of our more conventional one-ones, Barbara announced that she was assigning me the role of project manager for the company's imminent re-launch. Those dreaded words 'relaunch' sent chills down my spine as she spoke, and I cast my mind back to the catastrophic experience of the salon re-launch years before. I couldn't face another horrendous work event resulting in the destruction of my ensemble along with my will to live. At least with Barbara, I deliberated, there would be some excessive reimbursement fee or lavish compensatory attire if my worst fears were realised.

She continued to tell me how impressed she was with my efficiency and work ethic and stated that she had every faith in me being able to pull it off. Flattered and terrified, I accepted the mammoth task and for the next month, my work life was a blur. I strived to stay on top of my day-to-day duties whilst managing competing tasks of recruiting tech crew, and caterers, managing the guestlist, hiring and setting up the event space, facilitating the strategy and logo teams, ordering bespoke merchandise, designing gift bags as well as managing the budget.

Determined to prove myself and not let Barbara down, I stayed late for conference call meetings, reviewed mock-up design templates, and responded to emails after hours. I was going to make this a success no matter what; everyone was watching to see if the new girl had what it took, and I had to seize the opportunity and prove to them all that I did.

When re-launch day arrived, I was exhausted. As staff and guests began to fill the event space, my heart was racing. Barbara took to the stage, mic in hand, to deliver the welcome speech. I looked around the hall and admired the fruits of my labour. I scanned the smiling faces of the guests and the pristine layout of the décor and felt a deep sense of pride.

Later, the MD and the company partners congratulated me on a well-executed event. My first epic vocational feat, and I had emerged triumphant.

My success gave me a newfound sense of confidence. Life was good. I was excelling towards my ultimate dream, with features and bit parts in soap operas and films and was also winning in the corporate world too! I began to step more and more outside my comfort zone, and for the first time, at 27, with the encouragement of Barbara, I embarked on a two-week solo trip abroad, to my native Barbados.

This was a big step for me, someone who had previously had panic attacks at the thought of walking up the high street alone or would have been mortified at the prospect of eating at a restaurant unaccompanied. The trip was amazing and different to any of my previous visits to the island. I travelled the country like a tourist, visiting famous landmarks and embarking on day excursions. I went snorkelling and swam with the turtles (or should I say nearly drowned owing to my undiscovered fear of the ocean). I visited the wildlife park and ate saltfish burgers on the beach whilst relatives and friends worked in the day, and then in the evening they took me to local watering holes and popular night spots where we drank cocktails and danced the night away.

I returned to the UK, tanned, refreshed and liberated. I had a new mindset and perspective. No longer preoccupied with what people thought of me and who didn't like me or find me attractive. I had fallen in love with me, and that was all that mattered.

I vowed to start embracing things where I had previously erred on the side of caution. Typically, a homebody, I could spend an entire weekend not seeing or speaking to anyone. Pottering around my studio flat, I attended to random DIY projects and watching my beloved *Friends* video collection on repeat, but now I forced myself to have a more outgoing perspective. Allowing the extroverted side of my personality to take precedence over my introverted tendencies. I accepted dinner invitations and went solo to networking events and career speed dating sessions.

I went to art galleries and attended film screenings alone. I rekindled my love for roller skating and attended Friday night roller disco at the local nightclub with family and friends. I went to dinner alone and even attended the cinema by myself, being sure to avoid the Friday late-night showings, so I didn't look like I had been stood up.

I had always been chatty and sociable as a child and it felt like somewhere in-between then and now, I had lost myself. But now I was evolving, removing the years of self-doubt and inhibitions. I was shedding all my insecurities like layers of an onion, revealing my once uninhibited, bubbly, outgoing personality as I sparked up conversation with strangers at ease, waiting at the bus stop or on a park bench on my lunch break.

It soon became a running joke amongst friends and work colleagues that I always had a new face to introduce to the group of someone that I had met on a random outing or morning commute.

My years working at the ad agency encapsulated a real coming of age and signalled an evolution in who I was, and how I saw the world and solidified my recovery. But as much as I loved working at the ad agency and all its work-related perks, I couldn't help but feel like Clark Kent – living a double life most of the time, with the irregular drip-feed of TV appearances and random extra work on the side, I just didn't feel fulfilled and felt like my dream was taking a back seat to my work life, and so, for the first time, I questioned if I needed to shift the balance.

My 9–5 gave me stability and structure, but it was getting in the way of me attending auditions and being able to commit to casting calls and rehearsal times. I knew I had to make a decision. So, after two years in ad sales, I bit the bullet and told Barbara I was leaving. I thanked her for everything she had done for me, personally and professionally, but explained that I wanted to pursue my ambitions to become a TV presenter.

Surprised but supportive, she accepted my resignation and said she looked forward to seeing me on the big screen one day—No pressure!

This move was exciting, yet scary and financially daunting at the same time. I had always been so meticulous and cautious, planning everything out. Everything had always been done with precision and detail, leaving nothing to chance and thinking of every possible eventuality, especially when it came to my finances. I was measured and applied extreme due diligence, monitoring my spending, and balancing the books at the end of every month.

I never wanted to make a mistake that could set me back in debt or worse, render me homeless again—my worst fear of all. So, leaving a full-time job to bet on myself was going against everything I knew (I hadn't secured my next lily pad!). It felt as unnerving as jumping out of a plane in mid-air and free-falling to the ground, unsure whether or not my parachute would inflate just in time or if I would plummet to the ground, crashing in utter carnage.

I knew there was no way I could guarantee career success, so in the meantime, the least I could do was minimise the probability of catastrophic failure, and so whilst I waited for the outcome of the umpteenth MTV presenter search competition I had entered and received my 20th BBC rejection letter, I signed up to every major recruitment agency in London and accepted every temp assignment going, to at least keep the money coming in.

All the temp jobs were in media as I requested, production companies, post-production houses, broadcasting companies, and talent agencies. I felt close to the action even if I was on the wrong side of the reception desk. By God's grace, I always seemed to make a good impression and my agency frequently got repeat booking requests for me as well as several permanent job offers.

"It's a really good company and the pay is great, would you think about it?" My agent asked as he presented yet another corporate job offer, this time at a TV acquisition company.

I hesitated as I thought about my waning bank balance and the appeal of a good steady income for the first time in a year. But then, I contemplated what would have been the point of leaving a well-paid job in sales just to get another clerical job in a company where I could never realise my dreams.

"Sorry, Trent," I replied reluctantly. "It's just too far removed from what I want to do."

Frustrated, he accepted my decision and agreed to get in touch if he found something more suitable.

After hanging up the phone, I sat in deep contemplation, hoping I had not made a grave mistake and thrown away a potential lifeline. But there was something inherent within me that enabled me to believe that I had made the right decision, despite how bleak the present outlook was. Perhaps, it was my mustard seed-sized faith that convinced me to keep holding on in the belief that something better was just around the corner.

I reached down into that place that I had visited so many times before, when things went from bad to worse and looked impossible, and continued to believe, and then one day out of the blue, my phone rang.

When I answered, it was Kiera, another recruitment agent, who immediately said, "I know you don't want anything permanent right now, but I sent your CV over to the BBC and you have been shortlisted for a temp role there, would you be interested?"

My mouth fell open. I was speechless. "Would I?" I squealed, unable to disguise the excitement in my voice. "Of course I would!" I exclaimed.

It seemed almost serendipitous after years of applying to work at the BBC, writing letters to the heads of departments, executive producers and commissioners, motivated by my B, B, C A-level grades all those years ago. Despite the continuum of unsuccessful applications, I was undeterred from the notion that it was my destiny and that one day I would get to work there. And now, almost ten years later, there was a glimmer of hope that it might actually be happening. It was as if this had been what I had been holding out for all along.

As I arrived a few days later, in front of the White City building in West London, I stood in awe as I gazed up at the three iconic letters emblazoned across the front of what was otherwise a very ordinary building.

Once inside, I reported to reception and after a few minutes was escorted through the security-guarded turnstiles and up to the HR lounge on the first floor. As I sat awaiting my interview, it felt surreal. Regularly dropping off showreel tapes and cover letters at reception addressed to the infamous writers' room, I had now made it inside. Granted not yet as a presenter, but it was an in, even if it meant I would have to work my way up the ranks.

The interview was long and in-depth, with a written assessment, and a timed practical exercise, followed by a competency interview. By the end, I was mentally drained and exhausted. I had put so much pressure on myself and wanted it so badly that I felt frazzled now that it was finally over. As I exited the building, I felt a pang in the pit of my stomach as the doubt began to set in and I questioned whether I had done enough and if I would ever have the privilege of walking into that building ever again. I walked towards the bus stop to make my way home and just then my phone rang, it was Kiera.

"Congratulations, you got the job!" She squealed as I answered the call.

I froze on the spot, my eyes widened like golf balls in utter disbelief, my mouth wide open. "I did?" I quizzed in shock. And then silence. Kiera interpreted my unusual silence as dismay and acceptance and stated she would send over an email shortly with all the booking details.

Managing little more than repeated thank yous, I terminated the call and immediately called Mum. She picked up the phone and in an upbeat, inquisitive tone said, "Well…?"

"I just got a job at the BBC!" I erupted, my volume increasing with every word for maximum effect.

There was a momentary pause followed by an elongated scream on the other end of the line. For the next five minutes, we cried and laughed and cried some more as I walked the 20 minutes home, now too amped up to take the bus, besides I had a praise dance to do!

I was all set to start my new and exciting job in four weeks' time, whilst my predecessor worked her notice period. So, when Mum asked if I wanted to join her and Camille and some close family friends on a five-star, all-inclusive trip to Jamaica, I didn't hesitate to say yes.

Jamaica was amazing. We ate delicious cuisine every night, we hung out on the beach in the day, we swam with dolphins, we partied with the locals, we took day trips exploring the mountains and visited local landmarks, and Mum even helped us track down some of Dad's long-lost relatives and I got to meet a mass of cousins I didn't even know I had. My highlight was being reunited with Grandad M's lookalike brother, whom I had met all those years ago at the funeral and shared with him how much comfort he had brought me at such a difficult time.

The trip was everything I could have hoped for and was all the more sweeter knowing I had the promise of a secure and exciting new job awaiting my return home.

As soon as I started in my new role, I hit the ground running and was thoroughly enjoying my new and demanding role as PA to the department director. As I met the 60-strong team, I soon discovered that being 'green' aka completely new at the BBC, made me somewhat of a novelty, as people introduced themselves reeling off their lengthy, double-figured BBC tenures and revealing their unrecognisable photo ID passes, which depicted an image quite dissimilar from the one that stood before me.

It was a busy, high-energy department, with people always hurrying off to meetings and calling to request 'space in someone's diary'. I discovered that my line manager, whom I had not yet met, was on leave for a few days and I was relieved to be granted a few days' grace to get myself situated and make some headway with the extensive HR induction pack I had been given to read and complete as well as some mandatory online training.

Over the first few days, I received the odd email from my new boss, amongst the mass of emails that were steadily flowing into my inbox on her behalf. It felt strange managing someone's life and responding to emails on their behalf when I hadn't even met them yet. Then one day, she called. I instantly became nervous as my jovial, upbeat phone manner was met with a cool, direct response.

Not rude, but not friendly either. I jotted down her requests for me to arrange a few one-ones with her team leaders and to print some paperwork for a committee meeting she had in the coming days. As the call drew to a close, I told her I was looking forward to meeting her, she entertained some brief small talk before saying goodbye and hanging up.

In the coming days, the work intensified and despite my organised approach to colour-coding my inbox and keeping copious amounts of notes in my trusty notepad, I felt overwhelmed at the alarming rate in which my workload continued to grow quicker than I could clear it. Panic began to set in. I had waited so long to finally get here that I couldn't let anyone see that I felt out of my depth.

With my boss absent and me wanting to make a good impression amongst the watchful eyes of her direct reports, I felt paralysed in deciding who I could turn to just to simply ask a question or who I could trust as a sounding board in my decision-making, and before long the imposter syndrome began to set in again.

I started to lose confidence and question if I truly had what it took to make it in such a powerhouse as the BBC, or if I was just an invaluable cog that only served to complicate the otherwise seamless process. When I finally did meet my boss, my confidence continued to dissolve. She was nothing like I had imagined and from the expression on her face when we met, I could tell neither was I.

Collected and matter of fact, she kept the conversation focused and impersonal, always professional and polite but her tone conveyed disinterest and her smile never reached her eyes.

I became close friends with the other PAs in the department, and we formed a support network of sorts. We helped each other with administrative and technical support and relied on each other for information and advice. We lunched together and collectively looked to one another for daily boosts of morale and support.

On difficult days, we would steal away for brief chats whilst printing reams of meeting documents at the photocopier or find common ground as we shared frustrating PA-specific events from our day, whilst preparing teas and coffees for our bosses in the kitchen. The PA squad was an invaluable lifeline and truly gave me hope.

After my boss returned to the office, the atmosphere changed. There was very little chatter on what had once been a lively bank of desks where we sat. Sitting next to her, the atmosphere felt tense. My friendly PA buddies no longer stopped by for check in chats or to discuss lunch plans and I felt fraught with the never-ending demands of her team leaders who often made me feel like I worked for them as much as I did their boss.

Without addressing me by name or making eye contact, she would randomly begin referring to emails in her inbox, whilst I would halt whatever I was doing to frantically try and identify which email she was referring to with the limited information she had provided – searching my computer screen and trying to answer her direct questions without missing a beat, I often became flustered and apologetic under pressure.

Fortunately, my work spoke for itself, winning over the respect and appreciation of my peers. I was regularly commended by colleagues for my technical expertise or for my polished presentations or successful execution of a large-scale event. Senior members of staff would stop by my desk to commend me on my work and send me thank you notes via email. I was flattered that they all seemed to take an invested interest in the new girl, asking about my TV experience and aspirations, and expressing their admiration for my seemingly undampened positive outlook and unwavering ambition.

Three months into my six-month stint, at a department awards ceremony, I was completely stunned when I was awarded the 'Most Promising Newcomer' award. I didn't even know I had been nominated. It was an epic moment of recognition. One that I could immediately tell my boss was not willing to endorse or acknowledge, despite the 'Oscar-like', gold trophy proudly displayed on my desk in her direct eye line. One month before the end of my six-month stint, she informed me that she would not be extending my contract.

I wasn't surprised and couldn't help feeling like winning the award had somehow sealed my fate. I drifted off as she waffled on about the last few months being great for my CV and drowned her out as my mind shifted to my already initiated next move. When she finished talking, I graciously thanked her for the opportunity before returning to my desk to log off for the day.

I began praying that I would soon hear back from HR about the flurry of internal applications I had submitted in the lead up to this moment, knowing that it was unlikely that my contract would be renewed and that it was equally unlikely that I would want to remain in the role. Somewhat selective but more admittedly desperate I had cast my net far and wide, applying to internal jobs that may have not necessarily appealed on paper. But with the bigger picture in mind, I resolved that no matter what, I had worked too hard to get here and that just because I didn't have the endorsement of one person didn't mean it was over.

I was successful in acquiring two job interviews and by God's grace, just ten days before the end of my temporary contract, I secured a PA role working for two programme commissioners at the iconic Television Centre.

My first day at TVC in some ways felt like the first day working at the BBC. It was everything I had imagined working at the BBC would feel like six months prior, before entering into the White City building, which despite the amazing people and snazzy piazza, felt more like a trendy call centre than the historically enriched establishment that I had imagined.

TVC felt like hallowed ground and even as I entered the building and presented my staff pass, I half-expected to be called back by security and confronted with the sudden reality that this had all been a dream, and I was to be hauled back to reality as they politely escorted me out of the building. It was hard to hide my excitement as I walked below the bustling newsroom that suspended above the ground floor foyer, down the entrance corridor lined with dressing rooms, make-up studios and a hair salon.

I walked past the broadcasting studios and the intimate viewing galleries and along the long dome-shaped corridor, adorned with wall-to-wall imagery of famous BBC entertainers and TV hosts and scenes from some of the platform's most iconic programmes from its archive catalogue.

Memorabilia lined the audience café, a statue of Pudsey in one corner, a five-foot-tall Dalek in another, beside the gift shop a blue telephone box, which quickly became the backdrop for every photo op of every visitor and audience member that attended. Onto stage door, any time spent near here was guaranteed to yield a celebrity sighting and taking the lift up to the executive floor (where I worked) offered endless possibilities of a three-minute elevator ride in superstar company.

The genre commissioning offices were on the top floor and ran the length of the famous doughnut-shaped corridors: Comedy, Entertainment, Factual, Docs, it was all there.

Along the bright, sun-soaked corridor, mid-way along the stream of snazzy offices with frosted glass and beech-framed doors, I stopped in front of room 6045.

14

Room 6045

As I approached the door of room 6045, I spotted a middle-aged mixed-race lady with striking red, kinky hair in deep conversation with a 20-something slim white guy with his back to me. As I approached the door, they broke from their conversation and introduced themselves as Chantal and Mark. I extended my hand and introduced myself as the new commissioning PA before going inside as they resumed their private chat.

Working in room 6045 was comparable to no other life experience I had ever had before. The office was chaotic, and the atmosphere felt manic and lively all at the same time. The door was continuously swinging open and closed with a constant flow of commissioners, execs, and producers coming in to continue discussions from over-run meetings as well as unexpected visits of channel heads who wanted to hash out the finer points of a recent acquisition.

My bosses' schedules were out of control and managing their diaries and evening engagements felt more like performing the complexities of air-traffic control than general PA work at times.

Conversations and creative debates ran on and on with no sign of ceasing or reaching a mutual resolution until someone had to retreat and excuse themselves for an imminent meeting that they were already late for, flying out the door and down the hall, promising to 'reconvene' and 'talk offline' later—the infamous unscheduled 'later', a word that sent chills down any overrun PA's spine, as they searched the diary for a window and quickly came to the conclusion that there was no room for 'a later'!

Room 6045 was like a social experiment and demonstrated the direct result of what you get when you put a room full of opinionated, enthusiastic creatives in one office and leave them to hash it out. It was a room that embodied utter chaos and ingenious brilliance in equal measure.

In this room, worlds collided—a melting pot of people from all different walks of life representing every demographic of society: Black, White, Asian, bi-racial, young, old(er), parents, non-parents, straight, gay, female and male, working class, middle class, that room encompassed it all. Which was either designed out of sheer brilliance or the orchestration of some macabre psychology study as scientists watched behind a secret fourth wall.

Ultimately, this office dynamic guaranteed that no opinions were ever universal, and no decisions made were ever supported unanimously. A great democratic, self-governing collective, a dynamic that was admirable when observed from the sidelines and less profound when you were swept up in the thick of it. In essence, it was a shouty, busy, manic, brilliant, fun, draining, lively place to work, and the variable combinations of co-workers on any given day could bring about pleasant harmony or absolute discord.

Mark, the guy I had met in the corridor on my first day, sat opposite me. He was a project administrator for one of the commissioners I looked after. He was a shy but friendly type, soft-spoken and extremely intelligent, intimidatingly so. As the only other permanent fixture in the office, we soon became close allies— an unlikely pairing, we bonded and took comfort in our shared, bizarre experiences and cringeworthy goings on in the office.

Even more averse to confrontation than I, we would exchange raised eyebrows and shocked facial expressions over our computer screens as the creative conversations amongst our colleagues grew heated and voices became raised. Desperate to escape rising tensions, we would excuse ourselves for an opportune coffee run and escape, taking solace in the tranquillity of the corridor on the other side of the door. I soon came to understand why I had found him and Chantal there on my first day and it soon became a place we frequented together for a brief respite.

Mark and I made two and Chantal made three, in our unconventional friendship group. Chantal was the polar opposite of Mark, small in stature but by no means a shrinking violet. A mixed-race, half-Sicilian, half-Sierra-Leonian woman in her 50s, who described herself as unapologetically pro-Black. She was educated, well-read and well-versed in an array of subjects from history to politics, to race and religion, to culture and economy, the list went on.

She was a social brainbox and I found her fascinating. She was an activist and a thought agitator. If I had the Rosa Parks spirit, Chantal channelled the spirit of every civil rights activist and pioneer that had ever lived. Brave and fearless, she marched to the beat of her own drum. Not only did she refuse to accept the status quo, I would go as far as to say she got a real kick out of being a non-conformist and pushing the boundaries, a true rebel at heart.

Chantal was compassionate, genuine, and not a respecter of person, and would take just as much time exchanging pleasantries with senior managers and the Director General as she did with the postman and the catering staff.

Contrite in her opinions and views, Chantal remained open-minded and despite proclaiming that she was not a woman of faith, she still showed genuine interest in my beliefs and respect for my values. The only time I ever saw Chantal demonstrate zero tolerance was when it came to ignorance of equality and diversity. In this area, she took no prisoners and would call out ignorance and what she deemed to be privileged mindsets.

Challenging those to take responsibility to educate themselves on the difficulties and hardships of others outside of their experiences and refuting all claims of lack of awareness as nothing more than a cop-out.

As a result, Chantal was often on the front lines of spirited conversations in the office, fending off creative fire, and leading conversations about productions and their compositions, sparking debate around ideology, unconscious biases and representation.

In moments of office conflict, I regressed to tactics of avoidance I had adopted as a child. Growing up in a house of conflict and disputes, room 6045 brought up a wealth of unresolved childhood traumas for me and some days, I felt severely triggered and sick to my stomach at the frequency of slammed doors and creative blow-ups.

On a good day, the random pattern of colleagues entering and leaving the office allowed for moments of positive engagements and harmonious discourse as a colleague would lighten the mood with a humorous anecdote from a pitch meeting, or another would share in passing a talent spotting moment they had experienced in the BBC Bar at lunch. These unpredictable amiable instances often chased away negative residual feelings and replaced them with comfort and warmth.

My colleagues were bonkers but there was also a real sense that everyone cared, perhaps a little too much, but had good intentions at heart and were just passionate about the content they were making. I felt indebted to them in some weird, Stockholm syndrome type-way and felt overcome with a real feeling of comradery when I announced the news that my cosy, sacred, studio flat had burnt down in a building fire, rendering it uninhabitable. The entire team rallied around, offering to buy me new clothes and extending gestures of hospitality with invitations for a temporary place to stay.

After having my six-month contract renewed twice, I looked for something permanent that would allow me to expand and break out of the PA mould and more closely to the dream job. I applied internally for a job working in communications and events as a coordinator and got it. Up until this point, I had never not got a job I had interviewed for. It was an impressive winning streak, but I knew it couldn't last forever.

The job was great, less chaotic and more senior and audience-facing and my boss was a dream—friendly and bubbly with a no-nonsense, yet maternal disposition that was refreshing, although a little smothering at times. Her previous career ambitions as a TV producer made it easy for me to open up to her about my own TV presenting aspirations. I felt relieved and grateful for her unwavering support as she allowed me to take annual leave at short notice so that I could attend auditions and callbacks.

It felt great to not have to keep up any pretences. She knew that I didn't want to work behind a desk forever, but our mutual respect and budding friendship meant that she was assured that I would give 100% to the role in the meantime. In return, she gave me huge responsibility to elevate my exposure at the BBC; I got to produce events, coordinate talent dinners, write press releases and produce film screenings, and when I was off trying to realise my career goals, she was on the sidelines cheering me on, seemingly living vicariously through me.

15

Fractures

In a heart-to-heart with a close friend, about my journey on the fickle road to fame and fortune one day, I was expressing my frustration at the seemingly stagnant state of my career and the many setbacks I had experienced along the way. As we talked, I lamented about my elusive big break that seemed to constantly evade me and remain at all times just outside of my reach, beyond the figurative horizon.

And in her infinite wisdom, she replied, "I don't know if big breaks are really a thing, Nic! I think that only happens in movies. Instead, why don't you just focus on the little breaks!"

At this point in my TV career, I had experienced several momentary successes, namely one of the biggest was in 2010 when I won the MTV Ten for Ten competition. According to the competition guidelines I had to submit a 60-second video of myself presenting. I had the creative idea to create a one-minute news segment where I presented from a makeshift news studio (my mum's dining table) and then handed over to a reporter on location (also me) who then introduced the new MTV presenter (also me) who then did a quick piece to camera. My humorous and original idea and clever self-editing seemed to catch the attention of the judging panel and I was crowned the winner, battling out thousands of other applicants. As well as an impressive goody bag of kit including a handheld video camera, the competition organisers invited me and my plus one (Camille) for a tour of the MTV studios. Later that evening we were invited to attend a showcase of up-and-coming artists, hosted by the channel and were given full backstage access. Camille and I beamed backstage as we posed for photos with unsigned artists including Tinie Tempah and Ellie Goulding. That night we had the time of our lives, in what felt like an exclusive, underground music concert, where I was the VIP.

It felt great to reward Camille after all the sacrifices she had made in trying to help me realise my dreams; giving up her evenings and weekends to follow me to obscure locations to help me film content for my showreel. We filmed audition tapes, vox-pops, skits, and programme teasers; she even once helped me crash a street party to get content for a new programme idea I was pitching to a cable network.

Camille had long been my faithful confidant, production assistant, photographer and cameraman, and it felt amazing to be supported so valiantly by her. She was committed to the cause, even if that meant her having to zip my penned cues inside her sweat top whilst walking backwards and filming me at the same time as if she were a mobile makeshift teleprompter!

In my spare time, I spent hours learning how to build websites, script in HTML code, and use editing software to produce my content, resorting to self-help on account of my conservative budget. I negotiated discounted headshots for my website with talented photographers who were seeking to build their portfolios and hired film students on shoot dates who wanted to gain experience. I was resourceful, I was determined, and I was not willing to fail!

2012 was another exciting year, against the backdrop of The Queen's Diamond Jubilee and the London Olympics, my tiny breaks continued. I hosted the Images of Black Women film festival (a two-day festival, celebrating films inspired by the African diaspora), after pitching myself to a colleague I discovered ran a production company. A few weeks later, I co-presented on the main stage for The Afro Hair and Beauty Show weekend. I landed my own three-hour show on a popular West London community radio station and co-hosted Greenford Festival in the Park, along with an array of presenters and experienced DJs.

It was a whirlwind of a year and my hard work seemed to be making tiny ripples in a vast sea of opportunity. If nothing more, it felt as though I had definitely succeeded in getting my name out there, remarkably and to the surprise of most industry heads, all without the help of an agent. This was certainly not by choice, but simply by virtue of the fact that they all seemed more interested in signing known and established talent than fresh new faces in the industry. Conversations with potential representation management brands centred around connections, networks and social media numbers, and very little around actual talent.

I wondered what had happened to the days when agents were enthused by the prospect of discovering new talent. It was either an age-old myth or talent execs were no longer attracted to the appeal of acquiring such accolades and were quite content coming late to the party and jumping on the bandwagon of what looked like already established success. It was a frustrating quandary that felt a lot like the dilemma of the chicken and the egg, which one was to come first? And how did the unknown become known and how did the known transition from being unknown without being known? I couldn't figure it out. And so, I did all I knew to do and pressed on.

With every mini, momentary break, I became hopeful that it would lead to the ultimate breakthrough. But the highs of each latest career triumph soon dissipated and tailed off after a few weeks, as I became eager for the next thing to manifest. I found it increasingly difficult to not become discouraged in the interim when the phone had all but stopped ringing.

I was in a constant state of exhaustion, drained, having to think of the next possible programme idea or innovative way to package my presenting talent and unique ways to approach the same objective. Keeping creatively inspired and motivated felt like a 24-hour undertaking as I increasingly felt the pressure to keep the momentum going, fearful that my decreasing reserves of enthusiasm and self-belief would soon cause me to come to a grinding halt if I dared for one second to take my foot off the pedal.

During those periods, I became despondent about the future as my spirit became deflated leaving me with little energy to accomplish anything, much less focus on my actual full-time job.

To my BBC boss' credit, with the best of her intentions in helping me, she had successfully raised my profile amongst the bigwigs in her circle and I had gained great admiration and respect as an accomplished communications assistant amongst channel controllers and the head of TV operations.

But I soon learnt that my reputation preceding me had become counterproductive as I shared my elaborate future aspirations of a career as on-air talent over brief coffee meetings they had agreed to, only on account of my boss' recommendations. They appeared to struggle to share in my vision as they offered advice and expressed how hard it would be for me to make the crossover from behind the scenes to centre stage and warned that I would essentially have to start from scratch.

It was gravely disheartening to hear that all the career experience and mini breaks I had achieved externally thus far did not seem to compute as valuable or even usable currency inside the BBC.

Knockback after knockback, and a succession of dead-end conversations where I was advised to 'keep trying' and to 'gain more experience', only reinforced any existing feelings of frustration. I began to weigh up my options. My recent external successes had given me a glimmer of hope that maybe I had some discernible talent and that maybe, just maybe, I stood some small chance of one day truly achieving my dream. But for the first time, I began to contemplate the harsh reality that presented itself, that perhaps my dreams would never be realised here, at the BBC.

Friends I had previously worked with from the BBC College of Journalism attempted to encourage me in my career endeavours and during pep talks over crestfallen lunches and SOS coffee breaks, several suggested that it may be worth me considering doing a journalism qualification—something that the BBC's editorial and production execs would recognise and potentially enhance my resume in the competing world of BBC on-air talent.

I considered it but I struggled to even begin to get my head around the idea of going back to uni. It had been difficult enough the first time around with losing Granny within a month of starting my course, and then all the turmoil with me and Becks, not to mention bouts of feeling depressed, my hair falling out and frequently finding myself homeless. I had just about scraped through the first time, I was doubtful I would survive a second.

Not to mention I couldn't afford it. This time around, I would be enrolling as a mature student and couldn't hope for student loans and cosy halls of residence like times past. Plus, since the house fire, I was living at Mum's and needed to save so I could get back out on the rental market ASAP. Returning to my studies just didn't make sense right now. But I did have to do something. Because whatever I was doing just wasn't working.

After much deliberation, sleepless nights and soul-searching, I decided I had to give the dream one last ditch effort. So, without anything in the pipeline and no plan B to speak of, I followed my heart, against the advice of my head and resigned. I was voluntarily leaving the fortified institution I had fought so hard and for so long to be a part of. It made me sick to my stomach whenever I pondered on the gravity of my decision for too long, so I pushed it to the back of my mind as I worked my notice period.

Those four weeks flew by and before I knew it, they were over. There was no going back now. I had put all my chips in, I had spun the dice and bet on myself, I was leaving the BBC. My boss approached me as I cleared my desk and readied to leave. "Good luck, sweetheart!" She beamed, with tears in her eyes. "Go get 'em!" She said as we embraced.

Fighting back the tears, I thanked her for her generous gifts and unwavering support. As I exited the building, it felt surreal. I was so overwhelmed; I felt numb as I contemplated that I may have just made the biggest mistake of my life.

Temping was harder this time around. A lot of my old recruitment agency contacts had moved on and the pay wasn't as good as it once was. Previously being an agency favourite, I had the pick of the best assignments, but now I was back working reception and accepting anything I could get, just to maintain a steady income. To the outside world, I was living the dream and family and friends and old colleagues from the BBC would regularly message me and congratulate me when I randomly popped up on their TV sets in random and ad hoc appearances and when I sent them clips of me presenting online.

In their eyes, I was successful, after enviably quitting the rat race in bold and courageous pursuit of my dreams.

From the outside looking in, I was winning! But on the inside, I felt every bit of a catastrophic failure. Every day felt like a struggle as I battled my anxiety, insecurities and crippling disappointment that signalled the historical yet all too familiar beginnings of an emotional meltdown. I didn't feel any closer to achieving anything and it wasn't long before doubt and fear began to set in too.

What had I done? I panicked.

Had I just thrown my life away for a pipe dream that was never going to happen?

On the brink of destruction, I did all I knew to do, I called my dad. And just like every time before when I had called him, without hesitation, he raced to my rescue. Within an hour, he was at Mum's front door. He waited whilst I packed a bag and before I knew it, we were enroute to his house on the other side of town.

We had managed to repair our relationship somewhat over the years and by repair, I mean not talking about the past and glossing over things—the alternative, would have required deep excavation of the past and the life-altering, traumatic events that had plagued my childhood, and that would have been too much of an undertaking for me to invest in and for him to take. We both knew our relationship wouldn't survive it and so we avoided it like the plague and didn't talk about the past.

It was how I was able to reconcile with his former girlfriend, now wife, and be able to assimilate back into their home, despite my tumultuous ousting a decade prior.

Dad had missed so many big milestones and achievements in my life, but he always came through when I was down to nothing. Sometimes I wished he could have also been there to share in my highs too and to celebrate my achievements and not only witness the times when I had completely come undone. I wondered if he could be there even when I wasn't broken and didn't need to be put back together.

This time living with Dad and his family, I kept my distance, not wanting a repeat of the fallout from the last time I stayed out of the way. I could tell Dad wanted my stay to be permanent, but I was determined to make sure it was temporary and brief. This wasn't my home, and I was never going to be comfortable until I was back under my own roof, living on my own terms. I wasn't comfortable depending on anyone at this point, let alone for something as significant as somewhere to live.

I worked every temp assignment the recruitment agents offered, applied for jobs around the clock and saved every penny I could. The casting opportunities seemed to be drying up and soon enough, it felt like there was a shortage of temp roles available too. I was running out of options. It had been six months since leaving the BBC and it seemed like all the job offers sent my way by recruiters were opportunities to go right back there. It was ironic. I couldn't get in for five years and now it seemed I couldn't get away!

One day, I got a call from a recruitment agent who told me about a coordinator role in a project team at the BBC. The money was good, and the work sounded interesting and not PA-related, although it was not TV-related either.

"The interview is on Tuesday," she said when she rang. "Why don't you just go and get a feel for the role?"

"Ok," I replied hesitantly.

When she called a few days later after the interview to say I had got the job, I was relieved and slightly conflicted.

I had left the BBC with grand plans of stardom and here I was going back with very little to show for it and narrowly avoiding a catastrophic early mid-life crisis. I felt embarrassed and as though I had failed. But even higher on my list of priorities, above my pride and wanting to save face, was my need to maintain stability and to get a place of my own and so I accepted.

With the assurance of a new job, Mum and Dad agreed to top up my savings so that I could put down one month's rent and security deposit on a room in a shared house I had found in the newspaper. I think they conceded that having my own space was as much a priority for my independence as it was for my mental wellbeing. Grateful and excited to be back on my own two feet, I moved in immediately and slept on the floor for a week until my new bed arrived.

Surprisingly, it felt good to be back at the BBC. It was nice to see old friends and colleagues. In catch-ups over coffee and after-work drinks, I was open and honest about the fact that things hadn't worked out as I had hoped. I still wanted to be a TV presenter, but I couldn't take any more risks that would leave me in financial and mental constraints.

Several friends revisited the idea that I should do a master's in journalism as an avenue into the industry. I thought they were mad; I had only just come back. "How can I consider leaving again?" I quizzed.

One of them chimed in, "You could do it part-time like I did, it would take two years, but at least it means you could keep working here!"

"Just give it some thought!" Another friend coaxed.

I told them I would think about it and for the following few weeks, I did some light research on my laptop in the evenings after work, perusing potential institutions, curriculums and course fees. But every time I dug a little deeper and felt myself seriously contemplating it as a viable option, I became overwhelmed with all the logistics of such a monumental decision: I had rent, I had a car loan, I would have to leave my new job where I had only been in post for three months, to find another, not to mention I was almost 30, I didn't have two years to spare!

"Nope, I can't do this!" I remarked as I closed all the open internet browsing windows on my screen and logged off. But for some reason or another, in the days that followed, I kept going back, revisiting course pages that were now autosaved in my favourites and began to search for part-time roles in neighbouring departments. I looked up bank loans and began calculating what the minimum salary would be that I would need just to survive. As I felt myself coming around to the idea, I kept it to myself.

This time, there would be no big announcements until I had thought this through and had a watertight plan. I was terrified to tell my parents what I was pondering, considering they had just seen me go through one of the hardest periods of my adult life based on one precarious decision I had made, how could I muster up the courage to tell them I was in the process of plotting another!

I still had no idea how it was going to work, what I was going to do about finding part-time work or how I was going to pay the £9,000 course fee. However, despite all the unanswered questions, I told myself I would simply apply and leave it in God's hands. So that's exactly what I did.

A few weeks later, I got an email notifying me that my application was being considered and I was being invited to a telephone interview with the head of the journalism faculty at Brunel University. I suddenly really wanted it. I had always loved academia, but this was more than that, this was also the most positive I had felt about the direction of my career in a long time. It gave me a plan, it gave me structure, and it gave me anxiety! I flitted back and forth between feeling excited, optimistic and nauseous as I waited for the university's decision.

In the meantime, I searched the intranet for internal part-time job ads. Then one day out of the blue, a PA colleague I had confided in about my potential lifestyle change, emailed me to let me know a colleague of hers wanted to go part-time and was looking for someone to do a job share with. So once again, I bit the bullet and applied. *God, if it's your will!*

The week I found out I had been accepted onto the course, I also heard back that I had successfully interviewed for the job share role and found out that HR was finalising an offer.

I was ecstatic, although the not-so-favourable 70% salary cut brought me back down to reality with an almighty bump. After doing the sums, I was apprehensive and considered rejecting the offer and withdrawing my place on the course. My new income would leave me with nothing after paying the rent and my car payment, meaning all other expenses would have to come out of my overdraft or go on my newly acquired credit card.

I was terrified. But there was a tugging on the inside of me that against all my better judgement said, take a leap of faith, and so I did, I jumped! Freefalling into the unsure and the unknown.

The month before I was due to start my course, I found a waitressing job in a country club in the affluent Hertfordshire countryside and worked evenings and weekends to cover the shortfall of my new part-time salary.

Seven days before my 30th birthday, I found myself sitting in a classroom, attending my first lesson in journalism. It felt profound. I couldn't explain it, but I just knew in my gut the minute I walked in, that this was exactly where I was supposed to be. As I looked around the room as people made their introductions, it felt surreal. Surrounded by a mixed bag of mature students who were returning to education after over a decade, coupled with fresh-faced 21-year-olds who hadn't missed a beat in enrolling straight onto a master's course after completing their undergraduate degree just months prior.

For the first time, in that classroom amongst my tutors and fellow students, I finally felt like all my labour had not been in vain. I had hope that it was all coming together.

I had forgotten how much I loved to learn and being in an educational environment made me feel good. Initially looking forward to studying media law and learning Teeline shorthand—essential for journalist court reporting, I was taken aback by the intricate complexities and the staggeringly high threshold that the curriculum required in order for a student to achieve a pass. For law, we were taught by a qualified solicitor and for our exams, we had to memorise all the statutes verbatim and be able to cite an example of case law for each individual question.

Learning shorthand was literally like learning another language and then being asked to write it in hieroglyphics. The daily timed practice assessments frequently caused me to panic as I fluffed my transcript as I raced against the speed of the dictator, losing my place in the narrative or ending up with illegible text that was impossible to translate, resulting in a failed grade.

Ten years out of education was beginning to show as I felt rusty and out of my depth, in contrast to some of my young, bright and keen classmates. But I was undeterred, in fact, I was more determined than ever. This was my chance to change the course of my career, I had sacrificed so much to get here, and no matter what I had to do, I was going to make it work, failure was not an option.

So, I committed to studying longer and harder than most to overcome my challenges. Revising non-stop, practising with mock papers over the weekend and on my lunch breaks at the country club, completing practice exercises and downloading audio speed tests onto my iPod to complete whilst on my daily commute. I purchased every book on the reading list and spent all my spare time reading them cover to cover and making copious notes.

When the end of year results were posted online, I broke down with elation as I opened up the email and discovered that in my two law exams, I had been awarded two A's and I was stunned to discover I was the first person in my class to achieve 100 words per minute in shorthand.

As the first year drew to a close, I wished all of my fellow classmates farewell as they left university and readied themselves for graduation. As the only part-time student out of ten, I had another year to go.

After speaking to a career mentor, I decided to make networking at work a priority, as I thought about life after studies. And so, after several coffee rendezvous, several of which yielded very little fruit, a colleague put me in touch with her former boss, a news editor.

And following a carefully crafted introductory email, she agreed to meet for a quick chat. Too busy to venture out of the building, she agreed to meet in the newsroom in a 'meeting pod' just yards away from the famous BBC News studio.

She was polite, friendly and evidently very busy. She spoke in short staccato sentences, a style of speech I soon learnt was a universal dialect in the world of news, that conveyed that the person speaking worked in a high-pressured job and had little time to spare. I told her, in brief, about my career aspirations and about my course. Dubious at first when I mentioned that I was only halfway through, she asked me how many words I had in shorthand and if I had done all my media law.

When I told her my results, her shoulders eased and she paused in deep thought, and then said, "As you are part-time, there may be an opportunity for you as a freelance producer on some of your non-contractual days..." Her voice tailed off, as she contemplated the logistics of her proposal. Her expression conveyed she was attempting to organise her thoughts before speaking again. I sat gripping the edge of my chair, poised, unwilling to move or say anything that might distract her or jeopardise her completing her train of thought.

"Hmmm," she said, her eyes suddenly fixing back on me. "I tell you what, why don't you come in next Friday for a trial day and we can take it from there?"

"That would be amazing!" I beamed, trying to remain calm and collected, whilst doing cartwheels on the inside.

Detecting my undeniable enthusiasm, she interjected, "I'm not promising anything beyond Friday, we will have to see after that!"

"Absolutely!" I replied, desperate to vacate my seat and run off into the distance before more signs of my elation seeped through and she was tempted to withdraw the proposal altogether.

"Thank you so much!" I replied and shook her hand.

"See you Friday." She smiled as she got up to leave, distracted by a buzz and a ping on her mobile phone in her hand. We said our goodbyes and she rushed off and disappeared into the hubbub of the news floor below.

I sat there for a few seconds, paralysed in my seat at the realisation of what had just happened. I walked back to the entrance of the newsroom, taking in my new surroundings—journalists rushing back and forth, frantically typing at their desks and shifting in and out of meeting rooms, familiar-faced correspondents walking in and out of TV studios with scripts and crew carrying impressive pieces of kit up and down staircases in suitcases, with cameras precariously balancing on their shoulders. The feeling of the buzz of the newsroom was thrilling and intoxicating, and I couldn't wait to be a part of it.

That Friday, as I walked into New Broadcasting House newsroom, I was a ball of emotions. Excited, nervous, scared and grateful. For the first time in my BBC career, I was walking into the building, not as a PA, a team coordinator or an administrator, today was day one of being a journalist.

I was shown to my desk and introduced to the news desk team by one of the senior journalists. No sooner had I sat down and logged on than I was whisked off to the first editorial meeting of the day. Sitting in the back row of a conference room, with wall-to-wall journalists and an impressive VCR screen linking the room to BBC newsrooms across the UK, I sat in amazement as editors and producers discussed the news agenda and planned the day's output.

The feeling was galvanising. I was in love, and it was at that moment, that I decided I had found my niche, there was nowhere else I wanted to be and nothing else I wanted to be. I was sold.

I spent the rest of the morning fielding calls and updating the online planning diary, and just as my role as broadcast assistant started to feel disappointingly similar to my former PA duties, I was unexpectedly thrust into the deep end when I heard my name mentioned across the news desk and was beckoned over by a planning editor and several of her colleagues.

"How would you feel about producing the MH17 story for the one o'clock?" she fired off as I arrived at her desk.

I was speechless—talk about getting out of my comfort zone, I thought to myself! Trying to hide the sheer terror in my eyes, in front of a sea of inquisitive faces, I replied, "Absolutely, I'd love to!"

No sooner had I replied than the circle of editors dispersed, erupting in a chorus of 'Great!' and 'Well, that's sorted then' before returning to their respective places in the newsroom.

As soon as I got back to my desk, still in shock at the monumental commitment I had just made, the phone rang. I answered. It was the programme production exec. "Hi, Nicola, thanks for doing this," she exclaimed. "The missile expert is on his way and will be with you in 30 minutes," she continued. "The crew will meet you out on the piazza. I will drop you an email now with all the details!"

After a brief further exchange, she hung up. I took a deep breath as I hung up the phone and looked at my blank computer screen. This is what I wanted, I told myself, even if my moment to shine had come around a little quicker than expected. I had to do this, I told myself, as I attempted to psych myself up. Pushing down my bubbling anxiety, I sprang into action and told myself, that whatever I needed to know, I was going to learn in the next 29 minutes!

I prepared for the impending interview whilst trying to maintain the appearance of calm and collectedness as I made notes and drafted my questions, all the while attempting to ignore the feeling of nausea that was competing for my attention internally. Before I knew it, it was time!

The shoot went well, the expert seemed impressed with my questions and the programme producers and editors fed back that they were happy with the content as they scrambled to prepare it for the lunchtime news broadcast. As my piece aired live on the plasma screens around the newsroom, I felt an immense sense of pride and accomplishment. My elation only heightened when I experienced a drop in visit from the hiring editor who came over to see how I was getting on and she was met with celebratory updates from my colleagues of my morning undertaking.

As I got ready to leave that evening, the deputy desk editor approached me and passed on the message that the hiring editor had asked to see if I was free to come in again the following Friday for another shift. I didn't hesitate to accept. As I left for the day, I was utterly exhausted but euphoric. I had just experienced the most intense day of my career so far and emerged triumphant.

One Friday turned into another and another, and before I knew it, I had been working in the newsroom for over three months. I was constantly confronted with new challenges and situations that I was convinced this time I would not overcome and every time I did the elation was unmatched. As the pendulum constantly swung between fear and inadequacy to success and jubilation, my confidence grew along with my passion.

I continued to rise to the occasion and began to carve out a name for myself as producers and editors assigned me more responsibility, including the complex tasks of court reporting and producing live outside broadcasts.

I was doing it, I was living the dream—well kind of. All I knew was that as far as little breaks go, it felt like I had made quite a few!

The summer flew by and before I knew it, it was time to enrol for my final year at uni. The second year was much more production focused and having completed the fundamentals of government and media law studies, we were pushed to challenge our creativity in modules on newswriting and video and radio production.

For my video assignment, I applied all the theoretical teachings I had learnt in class and combined them with newfound production skills I had acquired on the job and used them to self-shoot and edit a three-minute short I had scripted, focussing on the Rio Olympics. After weeks of brainstorming my ideas, I got in contact with the facilities manager at Team GB's training grounds and after completing an extensive filming application was granted a permit to film on the premises and interview some of the athletes for the piece.

On the day of filming, the facilities manager met me at the entrance of the track, gave me a tour and showed me where I could set up my colossal amount of filming kit: tripod, boom, camera, and microphones. I began to set up my shots and to replay my storyboard in my head, whilst attempting to give the impression that I knew exactly what I was doing and to disguise any evidence of my lack of experience from intrigued athletes as they looked on.

Terrified, I approached the team whilst they congregated for their morning huddle, stretching whilst they sat scattered on the floor, whilst attentively listening to directions from their coach as he walked amongst the group, towering over them. As I got closer, to my amazement and sheer terror, I recognised the head coach; it was a former gold medallist. I gulped. Trying to hide the intimidation and fear from my face, I continued my approach.

With every step, I tried to formulate a plan as to what I was going to do when I got to the group. I knew I would regret it if I didn't ask him for an interview, so fighting back every inch of insecurity as I arrived, I introduced myself and asked if he would be willing to be interviewed on camera. The arena was silent for what felt like an eternity before he politely declined.

Professionally, I smiled and thanked him for his time. Humiliated, I walked the long walk back to where I had set up, to continue capturing my shots. Despite my very public humiliation, I tried to look unaffected and continued on with the day's filming.

It was nearing the end of the shoot when out of the blue, the famous coach approached me and, to my amazement, said in a cavalier tone, "Actually, I will do the interview."

I don't know if it was divine intervention or if he had just decided after lengthy observation that I somewhat looked like I knew what I was doing and was probably legit. But whatever it was, I was grateful. Leaving no time for him to change his mind, I went straight into journalist mode, setting up my camera, readying the mic, and with no time for prep, I started the camera rolling—Action!

16

When Doves Cry

It was mid-December and Christmas break was fast approaching as I turned my focus towards end of term assignments and was in the thick of completing my coursework submissions. I was especially looking forward to term two, where I was due to undertake a module in radio production. After that, 'school' would be out, and a summer of exams and the dreaded dissertation was all that stood in-between me and crossing the finish line.

Every time I thought about the colossal body of work that would be required at the final stage of my course, I got a lump in my throat. I had heard terrible things about dissertations from older family members and my peers during my undergraduate degree and had always felt grateful and relieved that I had managed to avoid it, doing a humanities-focused bachelor's degree. But this time around, there would be no escaping it.

This left me nervous and anxious as I pondered the mammoth thesis, I would soon be required to produce that would dominate my life for four months and eclipse my entire summer. In an attempt to distract myself, I chose to apply tunnel vision and to only concentrate on the present.

I had just secured two exclusive interviews for a story I was writing for my feature assignment. The piece reported on the lack of awareness surrounding the debilitating condition of sickle cell disease—a blood disorder that disproportionately affects People of Colour. Over the years, I had come to know several people personally who had suffered from the condition and so the opportunity to bring awareness to the disease with the use of engaging copy was a compelling prospect.

During my one-hour train journey to the rendezvous spot for an interview with a sickle cell sufferer, I perused my interview papers, tweaking questions and editing my notes as I went. Occasionally, I checked my phone, scanning my social media feed and scrolling through private posts of family members and friends as a welcome distraction. I flitted back and forth between apps on my mobile phone as the train entered and exited stations en route to my destination when a post by my aunt Alison caught me by surprise.

She mentioned in her status that the day before she had won a restraining order against a nuisance neighbour that had engaged in a two-year campaign of harassment against her and the family. I was stunned and instantly felt bad that I had no idea that she and my uncle and teenage cousin Kori had been going through such a terrible time. I made a mental note to reach out to her after my big interview and was comforted by her post which signalled an end to the whole traumatic ordeal.

I exited the train and made my way to the meeting point. I had told Mum and Camille about the interview the day before, so I was especially surprised and slightly irritated when Mum kept calling me right in the middle of my feature debut. How embarrassing, I thought, as I shifted my phone from vibrate to silent and apologised to my interviewee for the frequent buzzing interruptions coming from my handbag, which was now firmly placed under the table.

After the interview, I thanked my interviewee, and we parted ways on Oxford Street in central London before I headed to the train station. Just then, I remembered my phone buried in the bottom of my bag. I dug it out and switched the ringer back on as I entered the underground station. On the tube, unable to check my voicemails, I put my earphones in and switched on my music playlist.

An hour later, as I departed from the train, my phone regained satellite reception and instantaneously started buzzing and vibrating with an influx of pending text messages now arriving in my inbox. As I unlocked my phone to respond, my phone immediately started ringing. It was Mum again. I answered sharply, "Mum, I was in my interview, I told you it was today!"

She apologised and asked where I was. Still slightly irritated, I told her I was coming out of the station and would call her back when I got home. But then to my surprise, she informed me she was already at the station and would give me a lift. When I declined and said I was happy to walk the short 15-minute walk home, she insisted. So, to avoid an argument, I accepted.

I exited the station and walked along the windy footpath, up the stairs and down the hill where her car was parked on the edge of the retail park. Bumped up, the car was half on the kerb, the black gloss exterior glowed, bathed in the red fluorescent lights of the closed superstore opposite. On my approach, I realised that Camille was in the car too, uncharacteristically sitting in the back seat. Surprised, I chuckled and tapped on the tinted window at her, before moving towards the passenger door, opening it and climbing in. As soon as I sat down in the front passenger seat of the car and Mum turned to face me, my annoyance instantly evaporated as I noticed her eyes were puffy and red and that she had noticeably been crying.

"What's wrong?" I asked, alarmed.

"Something's happened," she replied, her voice surprisingly conveying she was more emotional than she had allowed her face to reveal.

I spun around to look at Camille in the backseat and suddenly realised that she too had been crying. She avoided my gaze, and I turned back to look at Mum.

"What is it?" I pressed.

Mum gulped, tears now visibly welling up in her eyes. "It's Alison," she said, her voice tailing off. There was a pause before she regained composure and said, "She was attacked this morning."

And then in a split second, my mind raced back to her social media post from earlier that morning before sharply returning to the present, and without missing a beat I screamed, "The neighbour!"

Mum's eyes grew wide, shocked at how I had so quickly filled in the blanks. "Yes," she nodded, wiping tears from her eyes with a balled-up tissue she had clenched in her hand.

"But she's OK?" I demanded.

Silence.

Mum lowered her head and looked straight ahead across the steering wheel and out through the front windscreen of the car onto the empty retail car park. Then suddenly, Camille's sobbing erupted from the backseat. Mum began shaking her head and then turned back to me, fighting back tears, she replied, "No."

It suddenly felt as if someone had expelled all the air out of my body in one instantaneous blow. My head felt light, and pins and needles began to course through my body.

"She's dead!" I shouted.

Mum slowly nodded, before bursting into tears. "She's dead?" I said again. I repeated it over and over, somehow trying to force myself to make sense of the words I was saying, but no amount of saying it made it real.

We rode much of the rest of the car journey in silence. A few hours later, we arrived at the family home. Friends and family gathered that night, in the beautifully decorated haven Alison had created, the Christmas tree already erected in the corner of the lounge, with wrapped presents beneath it and festive decorations all around, we sat in silence and in shock, as reality set in.

That evening, my dad and his siblings asked me to write a statement on behalf of the family. Hours later, we watched it be read out by newsreaders on evening news bulletins on every channel. It felt so strange to see her photo on the screen, her beautiful smile beaming back at us as correspondents talked about her in the past tense. Our beautiful Alison was gone.

No matter how many times they said the words, it still wouldn't sink in. Her presence still filled every room, her mug in the sink, her slippers by the door, her hairbrush in the bathroom. Murdered. How could this be?

Camille and I spent that first night with Kori and our uncle. It felt surreal to sleep in the house that less than 24 hours ago saw my aunt leave, headed to work as if it were a normal day and just a few hours later, we were going to bed there, knowing she would never return.

That night was one of the most haunting nights of my life, the sound of wailing and despair bled into the silence and chased away any hope of denial.

The next morning, I fended off press enquiries and requests for interviews at the front door and endured the dreaded death knock, having previously only experienced them from the other side of the door. It was like an out-of-body experience, watching the morning bulletins and 24-hour news channels broadcasting Alison's death at the top of the news agenda, correspondents holding up newspapers with headlines with her name and image emblazoned on the front page.

That day was one of the hardest days of my life. As a family, we experienced a tsunami of emotions that ebbed and flowed, caught in a cycle of shock, despair and disbelief, routinely set off by the arrival of every new mystified visitor and grieving friend coming to pay their respects. Despite a steady flow of well-wishers, there were moments when the whole house fell completely silent. The feeling of grief mixed with shock was palpable in the room and left a heavy mist in the air.

The silence was only momentarily broken by non-discriminant gut-wrenching cries triggered by a fleeting glance at a photo of her on the wall or the sharing of a memory of her from a happier time. Which would in turn set off a ripple effect of despair and crying, until there wasn't a dry eye left in the house.

The second hardest day was the funeral. A dedicated community board member, a conscientious colleague, a loving mother, a devoted wife and carer for my uncle, a fun-loving sister, daughter and aunt, Alison's multifaceted giftings, reflected for all to see in the reading of her tributes. In the weeks after her death, we lamented about her modesty and humility, her zeal for life, and her infectious positive energy. As we looked through old photo albums, we laughed through tears as we remarked on her outrageous and innovative fancy dress costumes and comical poses, always on an adventure and living life to the fullest.

Her ability to not take herself too seriously and lack of inhibition in the pursuit of fun and happiness had always endeared me to her, especially as a young, self-conscious adolescent, growing up.

My aunt Alison possessed all the qualities I had ever wished for in a big sister; loving, compassionate, kind, generous, fun and caring. As I stared at her beautiful image, captured in a snapshot, through blurred vision from my tears, I realised that for a brief moment in time, God had granted me the big sister I had always wanted. The only downside was that I wasn't able to keep her forever.

The third hardest day was six months later when we had to attend Alison's murder trial at the Old Bailey. We had just begun as a family to come to terms with the greatest devastation imaginable to our family and now we were going to have to relive it all again as we endured a harrowing and very public murder trial, and for the first time, I came face to face with the man responsible for taking her away, who had ended all of our lives as we knew them.

Returning to the Old Bailey where I had frequented for work, covering various high-profile cases felt surreal, as this time, I wasn't joining fellow colleagues in the press box, this time I was up in the public gallery as a 'family member of the deceased'; everything about it felt wrong. Combined with an added layer of anxiousness, I entered the courthouse, fretful that security, or the bailiffs, would recognise me.

I avoided eye contact with the court reporters as I sat on the balcony and tried to avoid the long lens of the press cameras as we queued outside each morning and again in the afternoon, as familiar faces of correspondents I knew, reported on the day's developments for lunchtime bulletins, just metres away.

Only a handful of colleagues knew about the travesties that had affected my family during those months and most showed discretion as I was granted compassionate leave and was graciously granted respite from the newsroom whilst they covered the story. I didn't want a spectacle; I couldn't bear the thought of further intrusion as journalists made the connection of the victim's niece being a broadcaster herself. It wasn't about me, and I didn't want anything to shift the focus from getting justice for our beloved Alison.

My nerves were fraught throughout the two-week trial, as I sat through the detailed accounts of witnesses, police officers and medical professionals as they relayed to the court what had happened that day. We sobbed as we heard her dying words recounted by those who were with her in her final moments, and I felt sick to my stomach as we heard the fatal and excessive injuries she endured.

During court recess, the family went to get coffee and I attempted to catch up on reading my course material and dissertation preparation. I couldn't believe that I was preparing for the biggest academic feat of my life and once again was in the midst of unthinkable, immeasurable grief.

In the coming weeks, old school friends from the local area and former work colleagues got in touch as they heard through the grapevine about the guilty verdict and sent words of comfort to me and the family. With everything I had left within me, I fought for my life. I fought to keep my head above the monumental waves and to swim against the overwhelmingly strong current of grief that seemed intent on washing me away and seeing me perish.

I used music as my therapy and discovered a gospel song called *Better Days (are coming)* and for two whole months, I played it on repeat every morning just to help me get out of bed while asking God to give me just enough strength to make it through the day.

Initially, a work acquaintance, Jan and I became increasingly close as she inserted herself into my life as a constant source of support and encouragement. She intervened and spoke to managers on my behalf and told me to go home when I forced myself in on the day of the verdict. Jan looked after me in those critical months, when I wanted to just curl up and give up altogether; as I struggled to be there for my family when I was barely keeping it together myself.

She encouraged me to progress with my dissertation when I felt like quitting and checked in on me by sending me texts and asking how I was doing periodically. God had sent me an angel in Jan, and I was eternally grateful. And by nothing short of a miracle, I made it through the final months of my course and submitted the dreaded dissertation.

A few months later, sitting at my second graduation ceremony, I reflected on how unbelievably fortunate I was to have survived one of the worst years of my life. When my name was finally called, I crossed the stage to the soundtrack of Mum and Camille whooping at the top of their lungs from their raised balcony seats, suspended above the main auditorium and was instantly hit by a flood of emotions.

I sat back down in my seat, certificate now in hand, and blinked in disbelief as my eyes tracked the words down the paper, and I caught sight of my grade— 'Pass with Merit'! I closed my eyes and looked up towards the ceiling. I sighed and exhaled, and in that moment, dared myself to believe that perhaps better days really were coming.

17

Breakthrough

I entered the new year with optimism and a newfound respect for life. My motto for 2016 was 'I won't complain!' Easier said than done, but it was a mantra I held dear, having experienced so much loss and heartache, I was committed to counting my blessings.

I was determined to focus my future on making a positive impact and living a life that was meaningful and intentional because one thing was for sure, it was certainly going to feel too short.

I enrolled in training at work and became a school mentor—delivering introductory talks on the world of journalism for primary and secondary school students. I was humbled and moved when after my very first session, a charming and inquisitive six-year-old pupil approached me and asked for my autograph. I affirmed that I was no one special but she persisted, despite my self-deprecating quip, thrusting her blank sheet of paper into my hand whilst telling me that my workshop session made her want to become a journalist when she was older.

My eyes welled up as a sense of pride rushed over me and I stood in deep reflection, marvelling at the beauty of the reality that in just one hour, I had managed to inspire such an innocent and impressionable soul. I thought back to Miss Kittow and wondered if she had any idea of just how much she had inspired me back then.

I joined the homeless ministry at church after I found it so rewarding volunteering for Crisis at Christmas several years before. I felt passionate about giving back and giving people a sense of feeling worthy. I knew only too well how it felt to not have a home or somewhere to call your own and what devastating impact that could have on your self-esteem and mental and physical wellbeing.

I empathised with how debilitating it could be to not have a job and steady income coming in. I understood the shame and the stigma that came with it and how out of touch one could feel as part of society—a slippery slope to discouragement and sometimes destruction. I wanted to extend myself to let anyone in that predicament know they weren't alone, that they were seen and that they too could start again. I had reinvented myself and started over so many times in my brief stint on earth, I wanted them to know it was never too late for them either.

Inspired by my sister's interest in deaf awareness and communications, I agreed to enrol with her on a Christian British Sign Language course. We would travel down to London every Saturday to attend classes and once qualified, joined the 'sign, praise and worship' team at church.

It was a year of many firsts and me pushing myself outside of my comfort zone, seemed to be where I felt increasingly more and more comfortable. I joined a local Deaf Club and attended alone, where I was the only hearing person in the group. We sat around and communed over tea and biscuits, and I soon got over my nerves as my new friends taught me new colloquialisms and abbreviations I hadn't learnt. I adapted quickly to the group setting, enjoying the welcoming atmosphere, and quick wit and humour of my new friends.

Travel was also high on my agenda and after living on a subsidised budget during my recent studies, I was determined to get as many trips in as I could afford, and the credit card would allow. I went on a girls' trip to Miami with Camille and friends. We had a hoot! Beach lounging all day and partying all night was pretty much the only thing on the agenda, although we did manage to get in a little sightseeing too.

It felt good to get away and to laugh and be carefree with Camille after a torturous 18 months, and our friends made sure that not a single moment was spent where we weren't having absolute fun.

That Christmas, we had a family reunion in Barbados, my first Christmas abroad. Determined to continue the liberated experience I had when I vacationed there alone all those years ago, I insisted we stayed in an apartment and vacationed like tourists. We went to beach parties, karaoke, and snorkelled amongst the turtles. On Christmas day, we got together with extended family and ate at a rented beach house right on the coast.

The following year, I travelled to Berlin, Amsterdam, Hawaii and Disneyland Florida for the first time. I felt like I was making up for lost time, —

2016 and 2017 were both epic years for gaining multiple stamps in my passport. Mum would often joke that out of all her kids, I was the one most likely to call her in the middle of the night from some random airport halfway across the world to tell her I had caught a last-minute flight to some remote destination on a whim and had bought a one-way ticket with no idea as to when I'd be back. I would fantasise that one day, I would be brave enough to do just that.

There was something so thrilling about discovering new places and immersing myself, temporarily in another 'world'. It was as though I was rewarding myself with that feeling of escapism that I had always craved as a child and young adolescent, now as an adult, it felt cathartic to be able to give myself exactly what I needed.

However, despite the acceleration in my personal and spiritual life, my career had begun to feel stagnant again and I couldn't see how I was going to make the transition from Fridays-only to becoming a fully-fledged, full-time journalist in the newsroom.

In the 12 months after graduating, I had applied to over 30 jobs and had at least one interview for every month of the year. But despite putting my best foot forward, my new qualification didn't seem to be making the headway I optimistically had hoped it would. After every interview, I either received a rejection email or feedback alluding to the fact that I had been unsuccessful due to the fact that despite exhibiting potential, I was lacking in experience (my intact interview success streak was over).

It was a vicious cycle. I needed a job to get experience and I needed experience to get a job. I was stuck.

I began to feel despondent and during a career rant with Chantal, she pledged to help me get some much-needed exposure by introducing me to her extensive network. And true to her word, within 24 hours, she had already sent out over a dozen introductory emails to her VIP contacts, where she raved about my potential and exceptional skills, urging them to meet with me and not to miss out on this 'amazing talent'—what great PR I thought to myself, as I perused her emails in my inbox and sent her back an email of gratitude.

I followed up on all the emails, introducing myself and inviting them to a coffee and a chat at their earliest convenience. One of the contacts that responded was an editor for BBC Radio and a week later, we met in a nearby coffee shop for the much-anticipated chat. A chat was never really just a chat, and this was universally understood in the industry, but was a less crass way of disguising the fact that you were asking for ten minutes to pitch yourself. A mentor once told me, "You never take a chat at face value, you prepare like it's an interview and then pitch your socks off!"

It was sound advice and something that has stayed with me throughout my career.

By the end of our brief meeting, where I had done my best to showcase my journalistic skills, he seemed impressed and after a quick pause, he suggested I come on board as a relief reporter on a freelance basis. I couldn't believe it. As he shook my hand and exited the coffee shop, I sat there in amazement.

As I left the coffee shop a few minutes later, I smiled and whispered under my breath, "The small breaks are turning into big breaks!"

Becoming a radio reporter was the hardest and most rewarding career move I had made to date. No longer chaperoned to outside broadcast assignments by crew members and producers like I had experienced working in TV, I had to learn how to deliver outside broadcasts all on my own and report live. It was a steep learning curve, but I was determined not to let my editor down.

I learnt on the job and within just a few months, my skillset had expanded ten-fold as I discovered how to operate outside broadcast equipment, record vox-pops, create programme trailers, write presenter scripts, file on location, report live, record pre-records and build programme schedules using BBC databases and content management systems.

Once dubious about switching platforms from TV to radio, I soon became inspired by the world of radio, enamoured by the simplicity of the medium despite the complexities in its production value, it maintained a personable intimacy and rapport between presenter and listener that was unique and appealing. I experienced real editorial influence when pitching package ideas and presenting original stories and felt validated by my team that I was making a valuable contribution to the output.

Radio was freeing, fast-paced and demanding and I loved it. In TV, there were always so many chains of command and I often felt far removed from the output I was creating, but in radio, there was an instant reward as I got to hear my packages play out live in the studio and hear the presenter read out the script and cues, I had prepared just a few hours prior.

The only downside was I only got to live out my dream job one day a week. The scheduler assured me there were no more available shifts every time I inquired, so disappointed, I resolved I literally couldn't give up the day job or should I say jobs! Influenced by my mum's relentless work ethic I had witnessed as a child, I kept pushing and for around a year, I was balancing four jobs at the same time—a three-day-a-week administrative job in BBC World Service, Mondays for BBC Radio, Fridays for the newsroom, and evenings and weekends at the country club.

I was exhausted but I couldn't afford to let the administrative job go until I had secured a full-time journalism role, I didn't want to go for a full-time administrative role and have to give up my small stints of utter bliss working in what I was convinced was my divine calling as a journalist. So, I juggled them all, until in 2019, I finally secured my first permanent, full-time journalism job at the BBC—four years after graduating and nine years after joining the BBC as a personal assistant, I had finally arrived.

That summer, I bought my first home. I worked out that by the age of 22, I'd had 22 addresses, so buying my first home at the age of 35 was even more symbolic for me than for most. It symbolised security, triumph and peace. For the first time in my life, I didn't have to worry about my homelife not being secure or stable. There were still a few missing pieces to the puzzle that I pined for. But this was a good start.

18

Adjusting My Crown

Chopping virtually all of my hair off was something I had thought about for a long time before I did it. My complex, love-hate relationship with my hair had gone on for as long as I could remember. My hair had always represented an area of my life I had not yet fully mastered or come to fully accept in its natural state. I was plagued with childhood memories of struggling with my hair texture and still had some of the emotional and physical scars to show for it.

I had scars on my knuckles from being burnt with hot combs, which burnt the nape of my neck and the tops of my ears. I had a scar on my leg from the time when I singed my forehead with the barrel of a tong, which resulted in me simultaneously releasing the hot poker, which unceremoniously landed in my lap, melting into my leg and branding the top of my left thigh. Despite my 'war wounds' and painful 'hair history', when I contemplated cutting off all of my hair, I second and third guessed my decision.

I knew I was tired of the expense, the discomfort and the time-consuming rituals it took to suppress the very essence of what grew naturally out of my scalp as well as the undeniable damage it was causing to the health and quality of my hair. But more importantly, I started to question what concealing my natural hair meant on a deeper level and what values it was subconsciously and internally perpetuating. Reflecting on the process of altering my natural self, caused me to question the impact it was having on my self-esteem and my identity.

Maybe it was an early mid-life crisis, or just a necessary identity crisis, but contemplating cutting my hair threw up many questions for me about my evolution: Had I fully accepted me and who I was? Had I come to terms with my childhood trauma and the teasing of my tormentors about my appearance and 'medusa-like' hair? Had I overcome my past and truly learnt to love myself, warts and all? Or did I still care what people thought of me and how society perceived me?

I am disappointed to say that even in this day and age, there is still a stigma around People of Colour wearing their natural hair in the workplace—locs, braids and afros are still perceived to be unprofessional by and large in the corporate world. Which is why it was ironic timing—when I decided to do the 'big chop', that my TV career was taking off and my 14-inch tresses were the longest they had ever been.

For some Black women, having chemically straightened hair or wearing weaves or wigs will have no bearing on their identity or feeling of 'blackness'. For others, make-up, hair dyes, and cosmetic surgery will be where they draw the line, perceiving these as deviations from their natural identity and for others still, nothing placed on or applied to their exterior would or ever could dislodge their deep-rooted feelings or affinity to their identity and culture.

Therefore, I need to insert the caveat that everyone's journey is different and that my personal feelings of 'selling out' (conforming and assimilating to fit in) were deeply entrenched in decades of self-hate and conforming to societal ideals of Western beauty standards, and that in my mid-30s, I had the revelation that I had not completely broken free from those shackles.

Cutting off my chemically straightened hair and starting all over again, from the root, with my natural curly coils was as much a physical transformation as it was a spiritual one. It had been so long that I didn't even know or remember what my natural hair was like. I was scared, and I was nervous, but I knew that to discover the most authentic me inward, I had to reflect this on the outside too.

I watched in shock as my transformation took place in the bathroom mirror. Scissors in hand, I grabbed and cut, and with every snip, a pang of fear leapt into my stomach as I was overwhelmed with anxious thoughts such as; What if I'm ugly? What will my colleagues say? What if people laugh? What if this ends my TV career, just as it's getting started?

Before long, it was done and there was no turning back. I stood staring at myself in the mirror in disbelief as I became acquainted with the unfamiliar reflection looking back at me. I studied my haphazard handiwork, examining my 'masterpiece' from all angles and running my fingers all over my almost bald head.

As the days rolled by, I began to adjust to 'life without hair' and to appreciate the natural beauty and texture of my curls as they slowly started to grow. I began to admire my boisterous and wavy curl pattern. I studied myself in the mirror daily, trying to embrace my new appearance. No longer able to hide behind my hair, I examined every feature, willing myself to find beauty in what I had once regarded as unattractive—my high forehead was regal, my blonde hairline unique, my dark eyes were intense, and my hair, well that was my crown, and I was going to wear it proudly.

I resolved that I was not my hair, but it was a part of me, and I was finally seeing it for all its beauty against a new backdrop of ideals. As time went on, my love-hate relationship with my mane began to blossom until it became a full-blown love affair.

Momentarily, I lamented for the little girl that had hated everything she saw looking back at her in the mirror all those years ago and I contemplated how different the course of her journey would have been if only she knew that 24 years later, she would come full circle, learning to embrace all those features that she had learnt to despise.

Returning to work was the most challenging phase of my transformation. It was one thing developing a deep appreciation and acceptance for my new appearance in the sanctity and security of my own four walls and amongst supportive family and friends, but how would my conviction hold up when I emerged from my safe cocoon of acceptance and was thrust out into a world of scrutiny against alternative beauty ideals?

Nervous and with palms sweating, I took the lift to the second floor and headed towards my department. Avoiding eye contact, I sat down at my desk, allowing my colleagues a reasonable amount of time to acknowledge my new appearance and adjust accordingly. Based on the fact that a colleague had recently transitioned from dyed jet-black tresses on the Friday to a natural silver mane on the Monday, with not so much as a mention, I figured a few minutes would suffice.

Unfortunately, I was not so fortunate and was soon bombarded with quips and indirect comments from across the open plan office that continued to increase in volume, making it impossible to ignore.

One male contractor shouted, "Woah, that's a haircut!"

I gulped.

Just then, a female colleague approached me at my desk and leant forward inspecting my tresses, and with a despondent expression said, "Where has all your beautiful hair gone?"

Taken aback and with nervous energy coursing through my body, I replied, "My hair is still beautiful, it's just different."

It was like an out-of-body experience.

The woman who had just responded sounded confident and self-assured, surely that couldn't have been me? I thought. I had surprised myself, as my statement did not reflect how I truly felt at that moment.

Trying to conceal the hurt in my eyes, I smiled back at my colleague, before turning towards my computer screen.

In more recent years, I have come to feel empowered by the 'naturalista sistas' that now grace our screens, appearing on daytime TV and primetime news bulletins, but when I started out on my natural hair journey, I could only look in the mirror for any true reflection of what I wanted to see on my TV screen. In the months that followed, I received many compliments on my natural hair from Black female colleagues and felt a real sense of camaraderie in the confines of the ladies' toilets or at the coffee machine as we exchanged experiences, and I encouraged them to go for it too. And as I embarked on this 'self-love natural hair journey' I prayed that one day, by seeing me on their TV screens, I would empower little Black girls all over the world to embrace their Black girl magic too!

19

Unprecedented Woman in an Unprecedented Time

February 2020 marked a pivotal time in my career. A few months earlier I had been responsible for coordinating a very important event for my department where I was responsible for producing a panel presentation of experts— showcasing my colleagues' expertise to a room full of editors and channel heads. My role had been strictly operational and not something I had planned on putting on my CV, due to the role requiring me to lean more on my historical administrative experience than my more recently acquired journalistic skills. So, I was truly shocked when a senior editor who had facilitated the event approached me at the end and invited me to coffee.

Excited and intrigued, I accepted and was pleasantly surprised when we met a few weeks later in the BBC coffee shop and he praised me on my stellar work ethic in successfully pulling off such a mammoth task.

I was even more astounded when he then leant back and asked me quizzically "Where do you see yourself, what do you want to do?" At that moment, he resembled some whimsical genie, readily waiting to grant me three mystical wishes. I paused, contemplating whether I should give the PC answer of wanting to develop and grow as a researcher in my current department or whether I should tell him my truth; that I felt I was being held back, that I wanted to be a fully-fledged news reporter and that I thought I had what it takes!

I took a deep breath and spoke from the heart. His eyes lit up as I shared my dreams and aspirations. Without pausing, I went on to detail my experience, my passion and my drive. This wasn't just 'a coffee', this was my moment, and I was going to cease it.

He listened attentively as I spoke, nodding as I shared my elaborate career confessions. And when I finally finished my 'pitch' I felt a sense of relief wash over me as I noticed his facial expression. Instead of looking as though I was delusional or that my goals were far-fetched or unrealistic, (I was familiar with that expression, I had seen it so many times before) I could see from his face that he believed in my conviction, and what's more, that he believed in me. My whole body started to tingle as I sensed something monumental was about to happen, and then in a very matter-of-fact manner he leant forward and uttered four simple, but profound words: "Let's make it happen!"

I was floored. He then went on to reel off names and connections he would explore in order to 'see what he could do'. I wanted to believe it, but I tried not to get my hopes up. After all, I'd had many coffees in the past that didn't amount to anything. I had sat in front of people before who had promised me in-roads with hiring managers and commissioners only to then ignore my emails or move on months later without as much as a goodbye. But there was something about this time that made me want to believe it would be different.

But even if I did have his full support, I thought, it wouldn't be that easy, and unfortunately, I wasn't wrong about that.

At the time, I was working in a role I was overqualified for and underappreciated in, with very little support and motivation from my superiors for career development. With that in mind, they should have been more than supportive of my career opportunity, but instead of paving the way they implemented roadblocks. It was at that time, that God turned things around, and senior managers who recognised what a unique career opportunity this was for me spoke up and authorised my temporary departure.

A few weeks later the senior editor (aka genie) contacted me again out of the blue and told me it was all arranged and that I would be working in the newsroom as a correspondent on secondment. I immediately went to the toilet and cried happy tears. I couldn't believe that diligently serving outside my area of interest had led to the biggest endorsement and most ground-breaking opportunity of my career thus far.

God was watching out for me again and giving me favour in the eyes of strangers, what a blessing! I was beyond grateful and excited, albeit a little nauseous when I thought about the prospect of broadcasting live on national TV. No turning back now!

On my very first day on call in the newsroom, I attended several fast-paced morning editorial meetings before being thrust into my first assignment. I had an hour to source a venue and interviewees as I was being deployed to cover the developing story of the tragic death of US basketballer Kobe Bryant and eight others in a helicopter crash.

As I researched the story, I became more and more disheartened by the harrowing unfolding details. Up until that point, I hadn't contemplated how triggering reporting on death and tragedy would be for me since losing Alison. Sitting at my desk I took a large gulp and tried to keep my composure.

I managed to locate a South London basketball facility where several Kobe fans had congregated for a tribute match. After a flurry of emails and several telephone calls, I secured an interview and clearance for filming, before running out the door, to meet my assigned crew and head to the location.

In the crew car, I scribbled away, tweaking my questions whilst fielding calls from the desk editor giving TX times and recce instructions. When we arrived on site, we had only 30 minutes to set up, which was made all the more difficult by the absence of a producer. So instead of me being able to focus on my script and the fact that I was going live to the nation in less than half an hour, I was required to book satellite space, run cables from the crew car, sort car parking and set up the shots.

On the outside, I looked calm and collected but, on the inside, I wanted to run away, as far and as fast as possible and not look back. But before I had the chance to begin to devise an escape plan, the studio technician in my earpiece began to count me in, "Over to you, Nicola, in 5,4,3,2…"

I had promised Mum as well as other family members and colleagues that I would alert them in advance of any broadcast assignments so that they could be poised with their remote controls to hit record and be able to save my TV debut as a memento. But who was I kidding? I had barely managed to finalise my script and swipe a stick of lip balm across my lips before the spotlight positioned above the camera was blinding my vision and I was confronted with the deafening sound of my cue being counted down and drowned out everything for the next 45 seconds.

I sighed a huge sigh of relief as the studio cued me out and confirmed I was cleared 'off air'. I remained poised, until they cut the feed, mindful that I didn't want any unprofessional rough cuts of myself on the editor's floor to later resurface on a blooper reel or some viral video platform in days or years to come.

On the third day of my assignment, I was assigned to report on the breaking news of the first two detected cases in the UK of a new virus called Covid-19. The information for this story was sketchy and the stakes were high, made all the more nerve-racking by the reality that the health editor and health correspondent were both tied up on outside broadcasts, and I had less than 20 minutes to prepare.

Before I knew it, I was sat in a brightly lit studio on the Victoria Derbyshire sofa, fielding questions, whilst holding a folded piece of paper with just two pieces of information on it, only too aware that I needed to fill a whole three-minute programme segment with my limited notes.

After the longest 180 seconds of my life, it was over. I couldn't exit the studio quickly enough. I honestly think to date that is still one of the most terrifying moments of my entire career and I was relieved when I returned to the newsroom floor to a hero's welcome by editors and fellow correspondents who had just watched the live broadcast.

But my celebrations were short-lived when a few minutes later, I was receiving calls from other BBC TV and radio outlets asking for me to 'appear' and shed light on what I knew. There was no escaping. But with every broadcast, I felt more confident, researching in the minutes in between each appearance and building my knowledge of the developing story and the details of this new virus. When the health correspondent stopped by my desk at the end of the day to congratulate me on my coverage, I was overjoyed and practically floated home.

In the following days and weeks of my secondment, I covered a range of breaking news stories for various outlets and felt a real gush of pride as my bulletin rang out over the airwaves of Radio 4 and I received messages of congratulations from family and friends. This was no small fracture, I was now in 'big break' territory.

I felt like I was on a roll. I was finding my niche. All those years of studying, pitching, and not giving up were finally paying off. I was in my dream career, and it turned out I was quite good at it.

Then a month later, the world stopped! It's crazy now to think that at the time when we were asked to gather in our boardroom and told by our director that we would be moved to remote working with immediate effect, I thought it would be a matter of weeks at most before we would return to the office and resume business as usual. Little did I know, it would be almost 18 months before I would see most of my colleagues again in the flesh.

Those early months of working from home were strange and unorthodox. I remember a not-so-glamorous occasion when recording a bulletin for Radio 4 on my mobile phone from home and repeatedly being told by the producer over email that my open plan lounge was too echoey. It will always bring me joy when I listen back to that particular report and remember the backstory, that I was able to get the perfect sound quality by recording my report under a thick duvet in my bedroom during the height of summer.

Another time, I remember being interviewed live on-air for BBC morning radio while praying that the postman didn't set the neighbourhood dogs off barking by his delivery schedule coinciding with my broadcast time.

Being at home did have some perks though. As a homebody I loved being able to spend more time at home, not having to wake up to my 5:00 am alarm or make the lengthy and expensive commute to London.

When the government introduced protocol around shielding and social bubbles, I isolated with Mum and Camille at their house. At first, it felt new and dare I say it, a little exciting; an all-week slumber party, slightly inconvenienced by the occasional Zoom meeting. But it wasn't long before the downside of the lockdown became a part of our reality: increasing workloads, longer working days, minimal time outside. Covid-19 dominated the headlines and the word 'unprecedented' became the most overused term for the next 24 months.

This phenomenon initially inspired heart-warming scenes of camaraderie and community spirit as locals lined the streets to applaud the efforts of NHS workers and window frames were decorated with tribute sketches of rainbows by children. But it wasn't long before the ripple effects of the virus began to trickle through—a relative of a loved one passed away, then a neighbour, then a close family friend.

Each story, more tragic than the last, with heart-wrenching accounts of families being unable to be close to their loved ones as they ebbed away on respirator machines, whole families being wiped out and health workers dying in service. Funerals online, speaking to elderly relatives in care homes through glass windows and being unable to embrace one another became the norm as the virus took hold in an unrelenting, inhumane and indiscriminate way.

At times, it felt like we would forever live under this big black cloud of grief, uncertainty and isolation and a post-Covid world seemed unrealistic and unobtainable. But as the clouds started to shift, life in this 'new normal' plateaued and I along with many others became more reflective than ever.

After six months of returning to the office and eleven and a half years at the BBC, I left. My last day felt like the end of an era. As I set my out of office for the last time and cleared my inbox, I stumbled across correspondences from colleagues old and new, those that had moved on and those that had passed on. I reminisced about room 6045, and about all the amazing people I had met, some famous for being on-screen, but others equally cherished for their hard work and diligence behind the scenes. I thought about my first day walking into Television Centre and how the last decade had flown by. I thought about my first day in the newsroom and the euphoria I had felt from finally having my dreams recognised.

I am in no doubt that period of working in the newsroom was pivotal to my career. Only God knew that within a few weeks of completing my attachment, the world would completely go on hold for two years and I truly believe that it is by His divine appointment that I was able to achieve one of the greatest accomplishments of my career before it did.

I will forever be embedded in this piece of history—reporting on the biggest global story of the century, and I am truly grateful for all those colleagues that He put in my path to make it possible.

After a difficult couple of years towards the end of my time at the BBC, I was so grateful to be leaving on a high. Having left my 'dead-end' role as a researcher, I had landed a journalism position the year before, in the coveted BBC disinformation team. My team were talented senior journalists; they were kind and supportive and I learnt a great deal from them, unearthing my passion for investigative journalism and writing.

I was touched when they would send me congratulatory emails and retweet my articles—debunking the latest conspiracy theories or unearthing the latest disinformation tactics.

Happy in my role, I was open to new opportunities but not actively looking, so it was quite by surprise and not even on my radar when the ad for my new role landed in my personal inbox!

It was scary to think about leaving the BBC after so long, but there was something in me that knew that I had to apply, I was ready for a change. I cast my mind back to what I had told my mum at the beginning of the year, that I felt that God wanted me to move on, expand my territory and my horizons and that I didn't think I would be at the BBC by the end of the year. And now here I was in the first quarter of the month, applying for an external job for the first time in years.

I opened the application and began typing. The new organisation was a Christian organisation, established and reputable—they had been around 175 years—longer than the BBC! The position was for an editor and media manager.

The more I progressed through the application, the more inspired and excited I was. The role was a dream and the organisation's digital offering was impressive, even through the eyes of a seasoned BBC journalist.

I loved their values and how passionate they were about evangelism and sharing the good news of the gospel. So refreshing. By the end of the application I was determined, I had to get this job! And do you know what? … I did!

As I walked out of the BBC's revolving doors for the last time it felt bittersweet. I had learnt so much here about myself both professionally and personally. I had found some lifelong friends and made some amazing memories, but it was time to move on. I was ready to turn the page and embrace the next chapter.

20

The Ugly Duckling Is Now a Flamingo

As I embarked on writing this book, I didn't give much thought as to how I would conclude my unended story. If I'm honest, at the beginning, I never envisaged making it to the end, due to the fact that for years I battled with the fear of sharing my deepest darkest secrets in print and being exposed by laying all my mistakes and past traumas out for all to see. As a result, I became paralysed by anxiety surrounding people's perceived perceptions of me and my 'faux collectedness' and poise, being dispelled by revelations of low self-esteem, bouts of depression and episodes of self-harm.

I was terrified at the thought of my family and I being subjected to merciless scrutiny for our past indiscretions and the stigma that is often attached to people who have experienced issues with mental health, violence and abuse. As a result, I held my story in, occasionally revealing small excerpts from various chapters of my life to provide the occasional colleague with a word of encouragement or to comfort a friend who was facing a similar situation, with a 'page' from my past.

However, no matter how much I tried to fight it, I kept coming back to the feeling that I had to share my story more widely and felt a sense of duty to inspire and empower an audience on a global scale. I had a burning belief that somehow this was the divine reason I had experienced all that I had and that by bringing my story to the world, to people from all walks of life, others could draw strength from it. And so, I finally succumbed to the overriding urge to put pen to paper and embarked on this journey of self-reflection.

As I did, I was confronted with processing and dealing with things about myself that I had never put under the microscope before. I was forced to relive and process unresolved traumatic events of my past, which has proven to be both challenging and therapeutic at times, made all the more difficult by doing it

190

during a time of working full-time in isolation against the backdrop of a global pandemic!

Writing an autobiography is not like writing a fantasy novel or a crime thriller, and every day that you sit down at your writing desk, you are required to revisit and unpick complex issues and events of your past. At times, the pen would flow and at other times, certain chapters would remain incomplete and untouched for months as I relived flare-ups of PTSD, followed by avoidance.

Perhaps if I had known how much would be required of me emotionally, physically and mentally, I would never have taken it on. So, thank God for not revealing all in the beginning, or you would not be reading the words on this page right now.

At the time when I decided to write the book, I was more focused on the beginning of my story as opposed to the middle which I guess is where I am now. The middle is the most pivotal, it's taking all you've been through and saying, 'So now what?'. So, I have asked myself just that during these closing chapters. 'What next?' As cliche as it may sound, it is 100% true that I am not the person I was when I started writing this book, and perhaps by the time you are reading it, I will have evolved again—I hope so.

I have had to reflect and re-evaluate how I process my life experiences and what that means for the future. It has caused me to assess my values, my beliefs, how I spend my time, what fulfils me, how I connect with people, how I deal with life's challenges and relate to them for healing and growth, but most importantly, it has caused me to seriously look in the mirror to see and accept every part of my reflection—flaws and all.

I no longer attach value to myself based on validation from others, accolades and praise, or compliments. Whilst all these things are nice, they don't define me. I have an assured understanding of who I am, and it feels truly liberating to know that I wouldn't want to be anyone else—not even the queen of pop! (No offence.)

How ironic and confusing it would have been to have continued to believe and accept others' reflections of me for all these years only to find that in today's society all the things they told me made me undesirable would now be perceived as favourable assets—being tall, with full lips, golden brown complexion, slim physique, high forehead, long legs, wild, curly natural hair! Please don't misunderstand me if you have none of these physical attributes.

The reality is that this is what is deemed hot right now by society and fashion magazines, and beauty manufacturers, but as it has before, this too will pass and that's why it's so important that we don't hold these beauty values so close to our hearts. How discombobulating it would be to allow your personal perception and wellbeing to be impacted by the fleeting, subjective, temporal opinions and attitudes of others.

Imagine trying to find value in yourself when everything is the opposite of what you are told: 'Great things come in small packages', 'The darker the berry the sweeter the juice!' 'Blondes have more fun!'. We cannot model our values for ourselves on societal ideals; they are fleeting, unfounded and flawed!

So today, when I look in the mirror, I see it all. I see my scars and my hurts, I see my joy and optimism for the future. I see unwavering faith and a zeal for life. I see a burning desire to positively impact the lives of others with compassion and understanding. I see that adventurous, courageous spirit that finds a thrill in challenging herself and pushing her limits. I see that Rosa Parks spirit, that is committed to advocating for change and speaking up and being a voice for the voiceless.

But I also see a child who suffered trauma and a young woman who suffered monumental loss and spent her early years desperate to find love. I see my vulnerabilities and a deep-rooted longing to be understood. I also see a victor, I see a survivor, who bears her scars proudly, as a reminder of having a 100% success rate at overcoming everything she has been through; but those scars don't define me, they just represent a moment in time. Thank God I don't look like what I've been through!

Sitting here today in the reality of my dreams, complete, sometimes seems unreal considering how my story began and I am under no illusion of how amazingly blessed I am. I thank God every day for all He has seen me through. Don't let this smile fool you, I'm convinced that those who smile the widest have oftentimes cried the hardest. And so, truly understand and cherish the value of a smile.

Overcoming trauma and mental anguish is not so much a destination as it is a journey. But it is empowering to say that I no longer feel as though the world would be a better place without me and that is huge for me. I have something to offer this world, a little touch of hope and kindness perhaps.

Today, I am learning to love my natural, chemical-free, curly, frizzy hair, not-so-skinny thighs and stand tall as the five-foot and ten-and-a-half-inch woman I am today (don't forget the half-inch!). But even more importantly, I am learning to embrace and love every page of my story. When I would tell people that I was writing an auto-biography at 37 years old, many people would ask how I could possibly have anything to say at such a young age, and my answer to them was as it is now—I truly believe I didn't go through my journey in vain and that the message I want to share is for others and is a timely one, for such a time as this. So, I hope it encourages someone—if I can do it, you most certainly can too.

The ugly duckling is truly now a flamingo—unique, radiant, colourful, uninhibited and unperturbed by the fact that she is not a swan, nor does she desire to be. Instead, like the flamingo, I endeavour to live my best life, true and authentic, unapologetically on one leg, just because I can, with no need for further explanation or acceptance.

Don't get me wrong, of course, I wish I hadn't had the traumatic childhood experiences that I did or experienced racism or depression or bullying, but every life experience has truly built me into the woman I am today. Were the wounds painful? Yes. Did they leave scars? Absolutely! How could they not? But am I healed? By the grace of God, I believe I'm on my way.

Some days are harder than others and it is a constant commitment to remind myself that I am worthy and that I deserve to be here when life's disappointments and doubts creep in. I forgive myself for those moments and accept that this too is part of my healing.

Revisiting historical memories from my life's archive to write this book has at times been difficult and on other occasions, I have surprised myself by how easily the words flowed onto the page.

As I reflect 'mid-story' (I hope I am only mid-story), I am excited to look to the future whilst honouring my past and all that it took for me to get to where I am today. By no means have I arrived, but every day I feel I am nearing my destination, in a more healthy, positive, optimistic way. I still battle with anxieties and insecurities like everyone else and it's important to remind myself that it's OK not to be OK sometimes.

I very rarely think about the past, but in writing this book, it has caused me to confront it head on. For a long time when I would get flashbacks, they would cause me to think about that little girl, with her broken spirit and shattered heart and I would lament, wishing I could go back in time and rescue her and make it all OK. But now, I remind myself (sometimes daily) that she made it; she survived and that she lives on in me, and 'Victory' is her name!

My beloved Kori,

We miss you so much beautiful. I'm sorry we couldn't keep you here and that what was on the other side was too compelling for you to stay. Oh, how I wish I could have changed it all for you and rewritten your story with the ending you deserved.

I remember when you were little, aged two or three and I babysat you, we looked through photos and I would ask you who people were and you would name family members, like it was a fun game. And every time an unfamiliar face popped up and had you stumped, you would scratch your little head and say, "Don't fink so!" So cute.

Another time I babysat you, you were no more than four, you woke up after your parents had left and screamed the house down for two hours straight, before becoming exhausted and asking to go lie down in your room. When I attempted to tuck you in, you said clearly, "I don't want you!" Fair enough, I thought, after that Camille took over the babysitting! Lol.

My darling cousin, I'm so sorry there wasn't more I could do and I'm sorry we couldn't give you a reason to stay. You hung in there, longer than most, and I pray God's mercy found you and you are cradled in the arms of the Creator, next to your mum.

I love you xx